Advance Praise for *Advocate to Win*

"Women are notoriously great advocates for others—now learn how to be your *own* best advocate. This deceptively simple yet incredibly powerful book will teach you how to respond rather than react, to use words as tools rather than weapons, and to focus on facts not just feelings."

—Lois P. Frankel, Ph.D., author of
Nice Girls Don't Get the Corner Office and
Nice Girls Don't Speak Up or Stand Out

"As an advocate for excellence, I am an advocate of this book! Heather's advice steers you onto the right path to actually ask for what you want, and how to actually get it. It's readable, it's actionable, and it's pure gold!"

—Alisa Cohn, #1 Startup Coach
in the World, Thinkers50 Marshall
Goldsmith Leading Coaches Awards;
Top 30 Global Guru in Startups

"This book shares how you can use the tools of a trial lawyer to persuade your Inner Jury to make the best choices and then persuade your Outer Jury to give you what you need to get exactly what you desire. The verdict is in—this book is a must read!"

—Sandy Abrams, author of
Breathe to Succeed

"Inside this book are ten tools that will allow you to become your own best advocate. Heather applies each tool to your Inner Jury (the part of you that chooses) and your Outer Jury (your friends, family, clients, and customers). The result is a primer on how to choose what you want—and get it. This book is a catalyst for your best future life."

—Petra Kolber, author of
The Perfection Detox

"This book provides the essential tools to advocate for whatever you want in order to get the life you deserve."

—Nir Eyal, bestselling author of
Hooked and *Indistractable*

"We all have a reason to advocate—for advancing our situations or for advancing those of others, for causes we champion or for voicing concerns of inequity, for our own needs and for the needs of others. If you want to understand how to ask more effectively and impactfully, this book provides you the tools you need—and the stories to understand how to use these tools—so that you can be successful in your attempts to advocate."

—Jill Schiefelbein, President,
The Dynamic Communicator, Inc.

ADVOCATE
TO *Win*

10 Tools to Ask for
What You Want and Get It

Heather Hansen

Post Hill
PRESS

A POST HILL PRESS BOOK
ISBN: 978-1-64293-663-6
ISBN (eBook): 978-1-64293-664-3

Advocate to Win:
10 Tools to Ask for What You Want and Get It
© 2021 by Heather Hansen
All Rights Reserved

Cover Design by Lisa Graves

The stories in this book are my stories. They involve other people's stories, so names, events, dates, places, and details have been changed to protect their identities and for literary effect. This book is not meant as legal advice, and nothing in this book should be construed as such.

Post Hill Press
New York • Nashville
posthillpress.com

Published in the United States of America
1 2 3 4 5 6 7 8 9 10

To my nieces, Brennah, Brielle, Bella, and Joey, and to my nephew, Jace. I can't wait to see all the ways you'll win.

Contents

Introduction: You Are Your Best Advocate

Life has so much to offer. Some of us go after it and get it. But for the vast majority of us—we just dream about what we want. Or worse, we're afraid to even admit we want anything beyond what we have. We just shuffle through the status quo, knowing there's more out there, but not knowing how to ask for it, get it, or even define it.

I'm not talking about big *things* either—like mansions or Ferraris. I'm talking about a new job or a raise. I'm talking about love or help at home or more time dedicated to taking care of oneself.

Is it wrong to admit we want those things? When we seem to have it all, is it wrong to want more? Maybe you want to start your own business or to finally go after a promotion. Maybe you want better relationships, more self-confidence, more opportunity, or more support. Whatever you want, it's perfectly normal to want it, and it's perfectly legitimate to ask for it. Not saying it out loud doesn't stop the wanting, either. It only makes it worse.

I know all about that. I know because I work with clients every day, helping them own what they want and then ask for it in a way that allows them to get it. I'm an advocacy coach. But I also know the struggle because…I've lived it, too. For years I didn't ask for what I wanted. I didn't own my choices, and as a result I didn't advocate for myself.

But when I finally began making better choices and advocating for those choices, my whole world changed.

I'm here to tell you that yours will, too.

For more than twenty years I advocated for other people as a trial attorney. I represented doctors, nurses, and hospitals in medical malpractice cases. It was my job to advocate for my clients, and I was good at it. When the list of the top fifty female attorneys in Pennsylvania came out every year, I was usually named on it. I was inducted as a fellow in the American College of Trial Lawyers. And I won most of my cases. Advocating for others was definitely one of my superpowers. But what I discovered was that I had an even greater superpower—teaching others how to advocate for themselves. I realized that when I coached witnesses on how to have the confidence and clarity to ask for what they wanted from the jury, we won.

That's why I became a coach. My coaching practice is built upon a collection of ten simple tools—the ten tools a trial lawyer uses to win. To win is to receive something positive because you've earned it. In the courtroom we won verdicts, but now my clients win support, attention, loyalty, and joy. They win money, love, time, and self-confidence. You can win, too. Once you start asking for what you want and getting it, your life will change. Once you advocate for yourself, your world will open up and you'll start collecting your wins.

Proof that this advocacy system works revealed itself over and over again when I worked in the courtroom. In court, the jury didn't really want to hear from me. The jury wanted to hear from the person who did the thing at issue. That meant I could advocate my little heart out for my doctors and nurses, but if they couldn't get up into the witness stand, turn to the jury, and advocate for themselves, we wouldn't win. The problem was that my witnesses weren't trained advocates. They were surgeons, nurses, scrub techs, schedulers, obstetricians, and primary care doctors. Stepping into the witness stand and asking the jury for a win often terrified them. But together, we turned each of them into an advocate and helped them overcome their fear and trepidation. They learned to advocate for themselves, with strength, grace, and charisma. And the wins poured in.

You might not think of yourself as an advocate either. But you are. An advocate is simply someone who publicly supports something. Have you ever asked your child to eat their vegetables? You're advocating for vegetables. Ever recommended a restaurant or a TV show? You're advocating for that restaurant or TV show. I bet you advocate for your children, your team, your employees, and your friends. I hope you advocate for yourself, your ideas, and the things you want. But if you don't, now you will. Because I'm going to give you the tools to do it so well that you'll get what you want, every time. I know these tools work. I've used them to help hundreds of witnesses advocate for themselves when the stakes are high and the pressure is on.

Too many people want someone else to do their advocating for them. My coaching clients struggle with this every day. When we first begin working together, they often say, "I wish you could do it for me." And if I could, I would. I love to advocate for others. It was my life's purpose for twenty years. But when you ask someone else to advocate for you, something is missing. No one else has your heart, your passion, your experience, your talent, your brain, your interest, or your charisma. No one else can advocate for you better than you can. And the sooner you recognize that you are your own best advocate, the sooner you can start using these tools to win.

An Ironic Epiphany

It took a perfect storm for me to finally realize that I, too, needed to learn to advocate for myself. I had to make some different choices and then advocate for what I needed to get what I chose. Before I realized that I could use these ten tools to ask for the things I wanted, and get them, I reached a dark place. It was 2015, and I had just finished a two-week trial outside Philadelphia. We'd won, but there wasn't much time for celebration. My car was packed with trial binders, exhibits, and suits for another trial, this one scheduled to be three weeks long and two hours away. I was sitting in my Toyota RAV4 outside the *Good Day Philadelphia* studios on Market Street, about to go in and do a television piece on a legal story in the news. Then I was to drive north, get settled in my hotel, and start advocating for my next client.

But I didn't want to.

And I was afraid to admit that, to myself or to anyone else. To the outside world, it may have seemed like I had it all. I often felt like I did! But I wanted to make different choices for my life and my future. I had a lot, but somehow I wanted something else, something more. And sitting there thinking that made me feel selfish and greedy. My life was full of gifts. I had a great legal practice, a fabulous condo in Philadelphia, a share in a shore house, and a charismatic boyfriend. Not only was I a successful trial attorney, but I'd also built a speaking practice and was doing multiple media hits. I'd traveled to Los Cabos, Ireland, and all across the United States speaking to doctors about how to advocate for themselves and their patients.

Despite all of this, I was unhappy. Trials are a zero-sum game. Someone wins, someone loses, and the results are public. I was tired of that. And I was tired of fighting. Trial lawyers fight for a living, and many lawyers enjoy the fight. That was never me. I have my psychology degree, and I enjoyed counseling my clients. I loved teaching them to advocate for themselves. And I knew that the counseling I provided and the tools I gave them to advocate changed them forever. But that was no longer enough. I wanted something different. I wanted more. And I was afraid to admit that, to myself or anyone else.

Specifically, I wanted to do more television. I'd recently started doing legal analysis for CNN, Fox News Channel, NBC, CBS, and Fox 29. I loved it. The first time I did live television, one of the producers said, "This is one of the scariest things you'll ever do." He was so wrong. When you're advocating for a doctor who has spent her whole life dedicated to helping people and now someone said she was careless when she wasn't—that's scary. Her emotions, her faith in herself, and even her reputation were on the line. And that scared me. But TV was pure, unadulterated fun. And the timing was great. There happened to be a ton of legal cases in the news in 2015 (anyone remember Jodi Arias?), so I had lots of opportunities to pursue this new love. But not when I was in the middle of a trial. I'd just missed two weeks of TV for the trial I'd just won, had a three-week trial ahead of me, and then another looming right after that. TV was on hold. I wasn't getting what I wanted. But I wasn't even asking.

My relationship was suffering from all these trials. My boyfriend lived in Connecticut, and he had his own career and a son. I usually went to see him on weekends because that was what he wanted. But I wanted more support when I was on trial. I wanted someone who was able and willing to come to me on those weekends. I wasn't getting what I wanted. But I wasn't even asking.

Then there was New York City. I'd wanted to live there since I was a little girl. Cities had always called to me, and I loved living in Philadelphia for many years. But I wanted the experience of living in Manhattan. I wasn't getting what I wanted. But I wasn't. Even. Asking.

Because I wouldn't admit what I wanted, I wasn't asking for it. And if I wasn't advocating for it, I couldn't get it. I was stuck in a mess of my own making. And those messes seem to hurt most. As I sat in my car that day, excited for the television hit and dreading the trial that would follow, it struck me that I didn't want to do this anymore. I didn't want to try cases back to back, with no break in between. I didn't want to win arguments for a living. I didn't want to be in a long-distance relationship with someone who couldn't be with me even when I was going through tough times. I had to choose something different. I had to believe I could choose to want more, whether I felt I deserved it or not.

That was the first step. Once I realized I could choose what I wanted, then I had to start asking for it. My life was made up of my choices. I had to make them. And then I had to advocate for the choices I had made.

I had an epiphany—I needed to advocate! My legal clients would come to me, tell me what they wanted (usually a win), and I'd ask for it. Most of the time, I'd get it. I needed someone to advocate for me and what I wanted. And that someone could only be me. I had to start advocating for myself.

The good news: I knew how. The tools I'd been using to earn so many wins in the courtroom could work outside the courtroom as well. Elegance, Words, Perspective, Questions, Credibility, Evidence, Reception, Presentation, Negotiation, and Argument. These were the tools that had allowed me to advocate for my clients so successfully. They were also the tools that my clients used to advocate for themselves and win. Now I'd use those tools to advocate for my choices...and for myself. I'd use those tools to win.

And I did. I started advocating for myself. Some of it was easy. I finally asked my law partners for help, and they gave it. I advocated my way to a lighter case load, which allowed me to do more television. In fact, I decided I wanted to be an anchor on television. Once I knew what I wanted, I found an opportunity that fit. Dan Abrams was starting a new network—the Law & Crime Network. I advocated my way into being an anchor on that network for a year. Then I realized that wasn't exactly what I wanted. I loved television but not talking about murder and rape all day. My wants changed. But I learned from that. I realized that I wanted to change people's lives by sharing the ten tools of an advocate. I wanted to reach as many people as possible, so I started a keynote speaker practice and advocated my way onto stages across the globe, sharing these tools with thousands through my speeches.

I wanted to write a book. So I did. I wrote *The Elegant Warrior: How to Win Life's Trials Without Losing Yourself*, and it became an Amazon bestseller. I wanted a podcast—so I started *The Elegant Warrior* podcast. Then, when the pandemic hit, I admitted to myself that after coaching my legal clients through trials for all those years, I wanted to be an advocacy coach. It took a pandemic for me to admit to myself that that was what I truly wanted. Quarantine helped me decide it was time to go for it full-time—not holding on to the security blanket of my legal career. Now I have a thriving self-advocacy coaching business where I help my clients admit what they want to themselves and then ask for it from others. It's the most rewarding work I've ever done.

But it didn't stop there. I wanted to end my relationship but also to remain friends with my boyfriend. That took some Perspective, Argument, Negotiation, and Elegance. That relationship ended, yet the friendship has survived. I wanted to move to New York, so I did—first part-time and then, in 2018, full-time.

My wants have changed. They've evolved with me and with our changing world. But I'm not worried. I have the tools of an advocate, and with these tools I know how to ask for what I want and get it in any situation. I know how to advocate for myself—with elegance. I know how to win. And that's what I want for you, too. I want you to want what you want and then go out and get it. The first step to getting what you want is being willing to want it. Then I want you to ask for it in a way that allows you to get it. The ten tools you'll learn in this book will help you do just that. You will become your own best advocate. And you will win.

Your Courtroom Cheat Sheet

In this book I'm going to use terms that are normally used to describe trials and apply them to your work advocating for yourself.

The Jury is central to successful advocating. In the courtroom, my jury is the twelve men and women I need to influence and persuade. Then, at the end of presenting my case, I'll ask them for what I want, and they decide whether I get it.

In life, you have a jury as well. In fact, you have two. You have your Inner Jury and your Outer Jury. They decide your wins.

Let's start with your Outer Jury, because they're easier to understand and often easier to persuade. Your Outer Jury is the person or people you want to influence. They're the people who ultimately decide whether you'll get what you're asking for. That means your jury changes with whatever it is you're advocating for. If you're asking for a promotion, your jury is your manager or your boss. If you want a new job, your jury is the person who decides whether to hire you. If you want to get a deal on your credit card interest, your jury is the woman from the credit card company that you're talking to on the phone. When you want better boundaries with a new boyfriend or his family, your jury is your boyfriend or his family. Every day you face an Outer Jury, and some days you face more than one. You need to know your Outer Jury before you can make them believe. Every time you have to depend on someone else to get something you want, that someone else is your Outer Jury. Throughout this book when I'm referring to your Outer Jury, that's who I'm referring to.

Your Inner Jury is a little tougher to imagine. It's the part of you that decides. We will dive deeper into the Inner Jury, and how you help her decide, in great detail in the Elegance chapter. Because knowing and persuading your Inner Jury is the key to advocating. You can't advocate until you believe, so you've got to influence your Inner Jury to believe first. And for many of my coaching clients, this is by far their hardest work. I give a workshop titled *When Your Toughest Jury Is You*, and it sells out. Women especially know that they often judge themselves and come up lacking. When you're advocating, that won't work. Your Outer Jury will never believe you, or believe in you, until you have persuaded your Inner Jury to do so. It's the first work you'll do in this book.

Every single one of the tools you use in this book has to be used with your Inner Jury first. As we go through the book, I'll describe how each tool applies to that jury. But you have to remember that until you have the jury inside your head persuaded, you can't persuade anyone else.

Once you know and understand the jury, you are on the road to winning.

Important Note: Advocates Win

There are, however, a lot of definitions of winning. In trials it's my job not only to win, but also to make sure my opponent loses. Trials are war. They're a zero-sum game, with a public winner and a public loser. As with politics and sports, someone always loses. That's hard. Fortunately for most of you, the things you're advocating for aren't binary. In life outside a trial, oftentimes, everyone can win. The definition of *win* that we're talking about in this book is from the *Cambridge Dictionary*: "to receive something positive…because you have earned it." The "something positive" is opportunity, money, respect, leverage, boundaries, joy, confidence…the list goes on and on. You earn it by advocating. You earn it by being your own best advocate.

Facts tell. Stories sell. Advocates win.

Many of my clients come to me for help with telling their stories. They know that storytelling is compelling, and they want to compel their bosses to give them a raise, their investors to further their investments, their partners to give them some help, or their Inner Jury to give them a break. While we work together to tell their stories, it's often not enough. Because what happens when there is a competing story? (And there's almost always a competing story.) You want a raise, but someone else at your office may be vying for a raise as well. You're telling your partner the story of how you need more of his time, but he's telling himself the story that he needs to work more. Your story reveals that you should get the investment into your start-up, but another start-up wants the investment, too. When there are two competing stories, the story that wins is the story that has an advocate. That person advocates with the right words and the right evidence. She works to gain perspective, ask the right questions, and build credibility over and over again. She listens and receives the information that she needs, and then works on her body language, tone of voice, and facial expressions to be sure she resonates as she advocates. This advocate believes in herself and her story.

She advocates like a trial lawyer. She wins.

The other reason that advocates win is that when you're an extraordinary advocate you always leave an advocate behind. That's someone who advocates for you and your "case" when you're not around. So, you will be using the tools in this book to advocate so skillfully that the people around you become your advocates as well. An easy example might be that you want to have a party for your anniversary and your partner wants to take a trip. If you advocate for the party to your friends and family effectively, they can tell your partner they want to party. You've turned the people around you into your advocates.

At work you can turn your colleagues into your advocates. If you want a promotion, you can be such a good teammate, such a good leader, and so effective at your job that your coworkers will urge your managers to give you that promotion. You can also turn clients and customers into your advocates. When you've advocated for yourself effectively, building credibility, using evidence, receiving as well as presenting, your clients and customers will sing your praises from the rooftops. They'll be advocating for you, and you'll have established the best kind of referral business.

You can even become so good at advocating for yourself that you turn your adversaries into advocates. I've done so. As I mentioned above, I'm a fellow of the American College of Trial Lawyers. It's made up of the top echelon of trial attorneys in the country. One cannot apply to be a fellow. Instead, someone has to recommend you, and then, unbeknownst to you, the attorneys and judges you've tried cases with or in front of are interviewed to determine if you'd make a good fellow. The very people you advocate against in the courtroom have to be willing to advocate for you to the College in order for you to become a fellow. In that case, the very people I've battled in court with advocated for me. I turned adversaries into advocates.

Here's a more practical example—a team effort that unfolded in the course of a case. I was representing an orthopedic surgeon who had performed a hip replacement on a patient who, afterward, had a leg-length discrepancy—her legs were two different lengths. That's a recognized risk of the operation. It happens even in the best of hands and when everyone has done everything perfectly. But here the patient said the doctor had made a mistake. We disagreed, so the case was going to trial. That meant the patient, who had moved to Colorado after the surgery, had to come back to Philadelphia and stay in a hotel for the two weeks that we'd be on trial. It also meant the doctor had to cancel all his other patients and all his surgeries to try this case.

We tried the case in the smallest courtroom in City Hall. I was seated at the far end of the counsel table, as close as possible to the evidence I needed to establish our case. Next to me, so close that our legs were touching the entire trial, was my client, the doctor. Next to him, at the opposing counsel's table but so close that their legs were practically touching, was the patient who had sued him. Next to her was her attorney, also as close as possible to his evidence.

On the first day of trial I walked down the long corridor of City Hall, pulling my trial bag behind me and practicing my opening statement in my head. As I turned to walk into the courtroom, I saw my client seated at the counsel table, chewing on a chocolate chip muffin and chatting with the patient who had sued him.

I scurried over and tapped him on the shoulder.

"Can I talk to you for a minute?"

We stepped into a quiet corner in the hallway.

"What are you doing?!"

He looked at me, confused and still chewing.

"I was asking her where she and her husband were staying," he said. "I recommended a few new restaurants they might want to try. And she was telling me about her grandchild's birthday party they're missing."

He was asking questions, seeing things from her perspective, and receiving information and evidence.

Over the course of the trial we advocated. I cross-examined the other side's witnesses, asking questions to challenge as well as to prove. I took the patient's story without taking her dignity. We built our credibility by keeping promises we made to the jury and meeting expectations we'd set. And when we couldn't, we owned it. We used evidence to support our case. My client and I used our body language, our tone of voice, and our energy to tell our story.

And every morning I'd find my client chewing his muffin and chatting with the patient who had sued him.

At the end of the two-week trial, the jury went to deliberate and very quickly returned a verdict for my client. We got what we'd asked for, and we'd won the case. As I was packing up my trial bag, I looked up to find the doctor once again chatting with the patient. At this point, we'd won, so I wasn't concerned. But I noted that the doctor had written something on a piece of paper and given it to the patient. As the doctor and I walked down the hallway one last time, my trial bag rolling along behind me, I had to ask.

"Doctor, what was it that you were writing on that piece of paper you gave to the patient?"

He answered, nonchalant as could be.

"Oh, it was my cell number. She asked if she could refer her friend and her sister to me for hip replacement surgery."

The doctor had advocated for himself. He won the case, and more importantly, he'd won her confidence. He'd done it with words, perspective, and questions. He'd built his credibility and used his evidence; he'd received and presented. In the midst of the war of trial, he'd turned an adversary into an advocate. Imagine what *you* can do.

With the tools in this book, you'll have the power to leave an advocate behind no matter where you go. You will get more of what you want because you will have more people advocating for you. Even your adversaries will jump on board.

What Would You Ask for if You Knew the Answer Was Yes?

Consider this: advocating is asking, but with superpowers. This book will teach you how to access and effectively use those superpowers. I find that my coaching clients have two different, but equally problematic, hurdles they have to overcome in order to advocate. One group is reluctant to advocate for themselves at all. They want someone else to do it for them. If this is you, the Elegance chapter and the Hire Yourself exercise are going to be especially helpful as you begin. But the other group asks for what they want. They just don't get it. And the reason for that is usually because they aren't asking well. They're demanding, whining, or implying. For those of you who can relate, the chapters on Perspective and Questions will be especially helpful.

No matter what your hurdle, I'm here to help you leap over it. It's time for you to start asking for what you want, and hearing "Yes," over and over again.

In this book I will share the ten tools of an advocate so that you can become your own best advocate. They are:

Elegance	Evidence
Words	Reception
Perspective	Presentation
Questions	Negotiation
Credibility	Argument

(Some of you may be wondering where Objections are. Objections are definitely one of the tools of an advocate, but they're covered by the others. Words are one way to object and handle objections. Perspective and Questions are others. You need Credibility and Evidence to object and to overcome objections, and Argument is for handling objections when all else fails. But for those who want to go deeper into Objections, there're three chapters on Objections in my first book, *The Elegant Warrior*. You can find those chapters and more on Objections at https:// advocatetowin.com/.)

You will learn how to use these tools with your Inner Jury and how to use them with your Outer Jury. Then you will discover that no matter what you ask for, the answer will be "Yes."

Do you want more money?

Do you want better relationships?

Do you want better boundaries, more respect, greater opportunities, better health, more magic?

You can get all of this and more by advocating for it. Though, there is one more caveat. You've got to actually advocate. Many of the clients I coach think the answer to getting everything they want is manifesting. They create their vision boards and do their visualizations. They ask the Universe to have their back and give them what they want. But they don't ask the person who can actually give it to them—their boss, their family members, their friends. It reminds me of a story.

It's the story of the man who is drowning in the ocean. He calls out to God.

"Please help me! Save me from this storm!"

Along comes a man in a rowboat, fighting the waves to get to him. When it finally reaches him, he turns to the rower.

"No! I'm waiting for God to save me!"

After fighting the waves for another hour, a motorboat appears in the distance. It approaches the man, and the woman driving urges him to hop in.

"Nope! I'm manifesting being saved by God!"

He continues to struggle and is losing strength and faith with each passing moment.

Finally, along comes a helicopter, with a ladder hanging down to scoop him out of the salty water.

"No! I know that God is going to save me."

The man dies. When he reaches heaven, he asks God why he wasn't saved. And God responds,

"I sent a rowboat, a motorboat, and a helicopter, you silly man!"

Same goes for the Universe.

If you're asking for a raise, you won't get it by asking the Universe. You've got to ask your boss. Looking for more respect or better boundaries with your partner? The Universe sent your partner for you to ask him/her. No matter what it is on your vision board, there's probably a person who can give it to you. Chances are the Universe has set you up for success, with your jury ready and willing to give it to you. You're on the brink of getting everything you want. But you've got to advocate for it.

Hire Yourself

If you're uncomfortable with this idea, with asking a person instead of the Universe, try referring to yourself in the third person. That's called an *illeism*, and it is powerful for advocating.

When you look outside yourself for someone else to advocate for you, you're giving away your power. But it's completely normal to want the outside help. At some point every one of my legal clients has said to me, "I wish you could testify for me." They know I have the training, the talent, and the experience to be an advocate, and they think I could do it better than them.

Many of the people I coach do the same thing. They look outside themselves for an advocate every day.

- "If I only had the right salesperson, my business would be booming."
- "When I find the right coach to tell me what to say and do, I'll get the opportunities."
- "I need a partner to help me get investors and then I'll be off to the races."
- "If my wife/husband would just know (fill in the need), our relationship would be better."
- "If my team was more like me, we'd be rolling in it."

All these people are saying the same thing: *I'm not the right person. Someone else could do it better. I need to hire an advocate.*

They're all wrong. You need *you*.

You are the best person to do all of the above and more. These are your ideas, your checkbook, your dream, your business, your product, your wants that you're advocating for, so your voice should be doing the advocating. Rather than hire someone to do it, you're going to create someone to do it. You'll create a different you, separate from you, who will advocate for you. You're going to use illeism to do so.

Illeism is the act of referring to yourself in the third person. Lots of successful people use illeism. When LeBron James said he "wanted to do what was best for LeBron James," he was using illeism. And he wasn't alone. Pelé, Andre Agassi, Julius Caesar, Salvador Dalí, Bo Jackson, and Charles de Gaulle all spoke about themselves in the third person.

Illeism makes us healthier and less hard on ourselves. In one experiment, people asked to speak in public were either told to talk to themself in *I* statements ("I can do this") or illeism statements ("Heather can do this"). Those who used illeism had a healthier attitude, performed better, and were less hard on themselves afterward.[1] Another study was even more interesting. Ethan Kross, a psychology professor at the University of Michigan, took fMRI brain scans of people who referred to themselves in the first person (I) and the third person (Heather Hansen). Using I activated the part of the brain associated with negative self-talk, while using the third person didn't. In addition, talking in the third person took less brain effort.[2] Illeism works. But it seems to work more often for men…

----

[1]   Ethan Kross, Emma Bruehlman-Senecal, Jiyoung Park, Aleah Burson, Adrienne Dougherty, Holly Shablack, Ryan Bremner, and Jason Moser, "Self-Talk as a Regulatory Mechanism: How You Do It Matters," *Journal of Personality and Social Psychology* 106, no. 2 (2014): 304–324.

[2]   Jason S. Moser, Adrienne Dougherty, Whitney I. Mattson, Benjamin Katz, Tim P. Moran, Darwin Guevarra, Holly Shablack, Ozlem Ayduck, John Jonides, Mark G. Berman, and Ethan Kross, "Third-Person Self-Talk Facilitates Emotion Regulation without Engaging Cognitive Control: Converging Evidence from ERP and fMRI," *Scientific Reports* 7, no. 4519 (July 2017): 1–9.

Although I've seen many examples of men talking about themselves in the third person, I have not come across any examples of famous women who use illeism. It may be that they don't do it, or it may be that they don't admit it.

This is a missed opportunity, though, because when you are getting ready to advocate for yourself and your needs, it's the perfect way to do so.

I have occasionally used illeism. For example, I was writing this book during the 2020 pandemic. For weeks I put off writing. Every morning I'd tell myself I'd write for an hour, and every afternoon I'd glance up from the latest TikTok video only to realize I had not written a word. Finally, six weeks into my shelter-at-home experience, I realized my plan was not going to work.

I had a talk with myself.

"Heather is going to sit down and write every day until this book is done. She's going to write a book that will help thousands of people advocate for themselves and their ideas. And she'll write another bestseller."

Speaking to myself this way made me so uncomfortable that I started writing to escape the discomfort. But I knew in order to make illeism work for me I had to find something else to do. Then, I realized something interesting about women. While not many women admit to illeism, some very successful women admit to doing something quite similar. They role-play. They pretend. They aspire. And they do it all with an alter ego.

The perfect example is Queen B herself. Beyoncé has Sasha Fierce, an alter ego she created when she was a young performer. Sasha Fierce was the one who stepped onstage. She was the one who got the criticism, but she also got the praise. As Beyoncé said in a 2010 *Allure* interview, when she didn't need Sasha anymore, she "killed" her.

"Sasha Fierce is done. I killed her. I don't need Sasha Fierce anymore, because I've grown and now I'm able to merge the two." Beyoncé used an alter ego to create a new reality, until she didn't need the alter ego any longer. She wasn't an imposter—she was aspiring. And look how that worked out for her.

Jennifer Lopez also created an alter ego (Lola) in 2009 and even gave her a Twitter account and her own website. But Lola didn't last long—maybe because Lopez already had J.Lo and Jenny from the Block, both of whom had done the trick. Mariah Carey has often referred to herself as Mimi. She's said that Mimi isn't an alter ego, but actually the truer person. But, as I tell my clients, that's the idea. Don't fake it until you make it, rather show it until you grow it. Your alter ego is the elegance inside you. Give her a name and let her out to play. Soon you won't need her anymore.

I give my clients some concrete ways to use illeism when they advocate. For example, one of my clients was working full time in a health care facility. Her hours were insane, and she had four children at home. She had decided to start a side hustle consulting for health care facilities, but she was struggling with asking for money for her services, with reaching out to old contacts to tell them what she was offering and with selling herself once she made contact. She needed to start advocating for herself, so she hired me.

The first thing we did was create her an alter ego. I asked her to write down all the traits she'd want her advocate to have. Her list looked like this:

Smart. Passionate. Classy. Charismatic. Sure. Polished. Well versed in health care lingo. Willing to let silences happen without trying to fill them. Great posture. Thoughtful. A good listener.

Once she completed her list, I helped her imagine a woman who had all those traits. We drew a mental picture of that woman, right down to the nail polish she'd wear and the way she'd wear her hair. My client named her—Sabrina. (She'd loved *Sabrina the Teenage Witch* when she was younger and liked the idea of her alter ego having a little bit of magic as well.) She worked on becoming her. The first time she tried, she faltered. She was in a conversation with a potential client, but when talk turned to money, she folded. When we explored what happened, she said the minute that talk turned to money, she forgot about Sabrina.

She needed a reminder—a transformation talisman.

Transformation Talisman

A talisman is an object thought to have magic powers. A transformation talisman helps you transform.

When I was a young lawyer just starting out, I was afraid to advocate. The first time I had to take a deposition, defend a deposition, argue a motion, or question a witness at trial, I had to psych myself up to be able to do it. And I used illeism. I recognized a Heather Hansen who wasn't afraid to advocate. In fact, she loved it. That Heather was ready, willing, and able to take that dep, defend that client, and argue with zest. In the mornings as I got ready for a day in court or a battle with opposing counsel, I'd say, "You're ready for this. You're prepared, you're excited, and you have everything you need."

But sometimes the self-talk wasn't enough. Sometimes I needed something else to allow me to step into *that* Heather. For me, it became my ponytail. For the first few years of my trial experience, I wore my hair in a ponytail every day of trial. I did that so often that the jurors noticed. Once, after a very long trial with multiple defendants, the jury wanted to speak with the lawyers after the verdict. They had questions about the case, the witnesses, the parties, and my hair. One of the jurors asked why I always wore my hair up. I told the juror it was easier for me to move around without my hair in my face. But that was only one of the reasons. What I should have told him was that my ponytail was my transformation talisman. It allowed me to be the advocate I wanted to be for myself and my client.

Another time I had a very contentious deposition. In fact, it may have been the most contentious and difficult deposition I've ever had. I was a young attorney, and the case was a bad one. The opposing attorney was one of the best attorneys in the city, and she was taking the deposition of my client. In the middle of the deposition, she turned to the doctor I represented and said, "Doctor, I'd recommend you end this deposition right now. Your attorney is too young and too inexperienced to realize the risk she is exposing you to in this deposition."

I objected and took a break.

Then I went to the bathroom to *freak out*.

Was I too young and inexperienced? Was I missing something? Or was she just messing with my head and my client's head because she knew I was young and inexperienced, and had a head that was open to being messed with? My Inner Jury was trying to decide between running to the elevator or walking back to that awful room.

I splashed water on my face and looked in the mirror. Then I took out a hairbrush and hair tie. As I put my hair in a ponytail, I started speaking to my Inner Jury, giving it evidence to support the decision I wanted to make. I whispered to myself:

> "You have got all the experience you need to handle this deposition. You will not let this lawyer mess with your head or your ability to do your job. You've got this."

I went back to reassure my doctor with confidence and a strong demeanor. Together, we walked back into the deposition room and continued without any additional drama.

Oh, and months later, when we tried that case, *Heather Hansen won.*

My clients have used a transformation talisman to great success. Remember Sabrina? My client decided that since Sabrina was a little witchy, she'd wear a dark plum, almost black, nail polish. Whenever that client knew she had to advocate for herself and her side hustle, she'd paint her nails that color. And I'm delighted to say that my client, and Sabrina, has given up the corporate job and has turned the side hustle into a six-figure business.

You can choose a transformation talisman, too. It could be a certain suit, a favorite pair of shoes, or a hairstyle. Or it could be a necklace or a pair of cufflinks. When I'm advocating for my clients in the courtroom, mine is the ponytail. But when I'm especially nervous about a TV hit and want to use my TV alter ego, she wears a certain pair of earrings. Just like everything else in this book, it's your choice. Whatever you choose, let it serve to help you to step into that inner advocate who exists inside you and start advocating.

It's Time

It's time for you to start asking for what you want, over and over, until you get it. It's time for you to build credibility, with yourself and others. It's time to gain perspective, use evidence, listen, and use your presence. The time has come for you to own your elegance and be the advocate you've been searching for.

You are the only person who can do it because no one knows what you want the way you do. No one else has the experience, the passion, the knowledge, or the desire that you have for your career, your relationships, and your life.

If you don't advocate for yourself, you'll never get that job, that raise, that promotion, or that opportunity. You'll never set that boundary or make that request. If you don't learn how to advocate for yourself, your life will never be what you want it to be. And until you advocate for yourself, you'll never realize the true extent of your potential. That would be a loss.

I wrote this book to give you the tools you'll need to advocate and win. In the chapters that follow, you'll learn that you need to build credibility. You can't advocate until you believe. And that means you have to start by believing in yourself. You'll soon realize that no one can do it better than you and that you have the power to turn everyone around you into your advocates as well. With the strength of your belief and the skill of your advocacy, you can even turn your adversaries into advocates. When you're finished reading this book, you will know *how to ask for what you want and get it.*

You will ask for what you want. You will get it. And you will win.

Remaining idle isn't an option. If you don't start advocating, you will lose.

Your ideas need you. Your bank account needs you. Your employees, your family, and your team need you. Your boundaries and your wants need you, too. You need you. You have your facts, and you have your stories. Let's use them to advocate.

Why? Because: Facts tell. Stories sell. Advocates win.

All you have to do is advocate.

You are about to learn ten tools of an advocate. I'll teach you how you can use them to persuade and influence your Inner Jury, and then your Outer Jury. I'll also provide you with precedent. In law, we look at other cases to provide us an example or guide. With precedent, I'm going to tell you the story of some of my clients and how they have applied these tools to advocate for themselves and change their lives. Finally, hundreds of readers of *The Elegant Warrior* told me they loved the "Summary of the Case" at the end of each chapter in that book. I'm providing the same recap here. If you read this book, do the work, and use the tools, you will become a better advocate. You'll start asking for what you want and getting it—today.

Precedent

One of my clients is in medical sales, and she had always done well. However, while she wanted to reach a higher level in her career, she'd hit an impasse. There were certain clients who made her nervous, and her new director brought out her insecurities and fears.

When I told her about hiring herself as her own best advocate, she liked the idea. And she loved the thought of creating an alter ego who would help her do it. She went to work. She decided her alter ego would be direct, confident, and sure. She'd also be funny, thick-skinned, and prepared for anything. She named her alter ego Caline and had one pair of particularly high heels she wore as a transformation talisman. Caline has served my client well. In our time together she's won numerous awards for selling, earned a promotion, and most importantly, she finally sees that there's no one better suited to ask for what she wants than herself (with Caline's help).

Summary of the Case: Introduction

1. *You are your own best advocate.* There is no one who can do advocate for you better than you can. And there is no better time to start than now.
2. *Use illeism to your advantage.* Whether you refer to yourself in the third person or you use an alter ego, find a way to remove yourself from the situation enough to advocate with ease.

3. *Try a transformation talisman.* Find something tangible that allows you to step into your role as an advocate and to be the best advocate you can be.

Chapter 1
Elegance

Choose your way to your highest potential.

Words are one of the tools of an advocate. That means it is important that you understand the meanings of the words you use. Looking at the origin of words helps me to get a deeper understanding of how I can use them to work for me.

The root of the word *elegance* is "to choose."

Your elegance is the part of you that makes the best choices.

Since your Inner Jury is the part of you that chooses, when your Inner Jury is doing her job well and choosing the things that will help you to reach your highest potential, your life is full of wins.

But your Inner Jury relies on your elegance for clarity.

Know What You Want

When I was practicing law, at the first meeting with a client I would sit down and ask them what they wanted from me and from the case. Did they want to fight tooth and nail to win? Or did they want to settle? Would they choose losing weeks with their patients in their medical practice in order to win the case? Or would they choose to sacrifice a "win" in order to do what they loved? The choice was different for every client. And often the choice changed during the course of a case. But I found that when we were intentional about the choice, talking about the pros and cons and making the doctor aware that he was choosing, we got better results.

Many of my clients earned peace of mind, time with their patients, and less stress by choosing to settle. That's a win. And others earned the thrill of a defense verdict and the satisfaction of feeling vindicated by choosing to go to trial. Either way, the wins were sweetest when the doctors were clear on what they wanted.

And the same is true, now, for the clients I coach. They can't start advocating for something until they know what they want. Neither can you. That skill—knowing what you want and what serves your highest potential is in fact your elegance. Once you know what you want, your Inner Jury can make the daily choices necessary to get you there. If you don't know what you want, the Inner Jury gets confused. Making clear choices and making *your* choices clear is part of owning your elegance.

It is sometimes difficult to identify what we want. I remember that feeling well. When I sat in front of the *Good Day Philadelphia* studios and cried, I didn't actually know what I wanted—not exactly. I could have told you what I didn't want, with great clarity and specificity. I didn't want to try so many cases. I didn't want a partner who needed me to be with him full time. I didn't want to live in Philadelphia forever. But admitting what I did want—to be on television, an independent partner, a move to New York City—took a lot more. Admitting that to my-self was one thing. Asking others for what I wanted came later. You need to be able to admit what you want to yourself first, too.

There's an exercise that helps people figure this out. It takes twenty minutes a day, for a week. Give it a try this week.

Every morning, right when you wake up and before you look at your phone or talk to anyone else, write two full pages in a notebook. Let the words bubble up inside you and then write them down. Answer the following questions on the specific days:

> Monday and Tuesday, ask: What do I want?
> Wednesday and Thursday, ask: What delights me?
> Friday and Saturday, ask: What works for me?
> By Sunday, take a look at your answers and you'll start to see
> your elegance. It will reveal itself in your answers.

Let's go through these one by one for some clarity.

What do I want?

When most of my clients first start asking themselves that question, their answers often reflect what others want. "I want to be successful." What is success and whose version of success are we talking about? "I want my children/spouse/partner/family to be happy." What does happiness mean to them? "I want to be able to pay for my children's college education."

Then they often go to twisted versions of what they don't want. "I want to feel better," or "I want to stop worrying about what others think or say." I often hear, "I want to stop drinking every night."

It takes about two pages of daily notes for them to get to the good stuff.

"I want to spend more time with my children."

"I want to learn to surf."

"I want to start a podcast."

The reason that we do this for two days in a row is that over the course of the day things that you want will pop into your mind. For many of my clients it's like they've opened up a dam and suddenly things they want come flooding out of their consciousness. You want that flood. Your elegance lies somewhere in those waters.

What delights me?

This question will help you to go even deeper into what you want. Because what delights you often points an arrow to what you want. Going on television delighted me. I was delighted when I got the call, when I hopped on the train to New York, when I got my hair and makeup done, and when they put the microphone on my dress. Every minute of every TV hit was pure delight.

For some of my coaching clients, playing with their dogs delights them. For others it's swimming in the ocean, working in the garden, going to parties, or having sex. Don't be afraid to admit what delights you and to want more of that in your life. Delight is important, and the more often you feel delight, the closer you'll come to your elegance.

What works for me?

Remember that one-size shoe does not fit all. What works for me might not work for you. I'm a single woman. I don't have children to worry about, and I have few distractions that I haven't chosen. My life is pretty structured and unencumbered. There are a lot of things that work for me that will never work for a mom of three young kids. Really think about how your wants will work into your specific life.

And even two different moms will have different things that work for them. They want different things. Different things delight them. If you spend your life trying to get what you want by doing what works for someone else, you miss the opportunity to get what works for you. Write what works for you without judging yourself. Maybe hard morning workouts work for you. Or maybe long strolls with the dog work for you. Perhaps it works for you to work weekends and have more flexibility during the week. Or maybe you take your weekends completely off to recharge. Own what works for you. Because it works. For you.

Schedule is something a lot of clients struggle with. One client read all the books and studies that say early risers are more successful. And she knew, from attending one of my workshops, that I am an early riser. She told herself she should be an early riser as well. And she tried so hard! But she just couldn't get herself to go to bed before eleven o'clock, and then she couldn't force herself up and awake at five in the morning. Before we started working together, she tortured herself trying. She called herself weak and convinced herself she'd never reach her highest potential. But her highest potential was her elegance. Her elegance was the part that worked for her. Once she did this exercise and realized that she was at her best later in the evening, she gave up this idea of being an early bird. She stopped beating herself up and started loving her schedule. And when she did, she collected more wins.

Answering these questions and knowing your wants will lead you to your elegance because some inner part of you knows your highest potential and how to get there. But you have to believe in that highest potential, that elegance.

The Angel Inside

Your elegance is the angel inside you. You have to see it to help you understand your elegance.

One of my favorite quotes is from the artist Michelangelo talking about his statue of David: "I saw the angel in the marble, and I carved until I set him free."

David is the Biblical underdog hero, the one who killed a giant with a stone and a slingshot. And the story of that statue is worth telling as we explore owning our elegance. In 1464 the Opera del Duomo commissioned Agostino di Duccio to carve a statue of David for the Cathedral of Florence from a six-ton block of marble. Agostino quit. Antonio Rossellino took up the task in 1475, but he, too, quit. Both men quit because they felt the marble had too many *taroli*, or imperfections. For twenty-five years this block of "imperfect" marble lay in a courtyard, a hunk of untouched potential.

In 1500 the decision was made to try again, and a number of artists were considered, including Leonardo da Vinci. Ultimately the commission was given to twenty-six-year-old Michelangelo.

He was given the block of marble and the opportunity to carve it. Michelangelo went to work. He carved in the open courtyard for years, sleeping under the stars with his clothes and boots on and rarely stopping to eat.

Prior renderings of David had shown him after he had killed Goliath, standing over the giant's dead body and often over his severed head, but Michelangelo chose to portray David before the battle.[3] His weapon, the slingshot he carries for battle, is barely discernible over his shoulder. David appears to be confident and concentrating. He is the Elegant Warrior, indeed. Michelangelo just had to carve away the imperfections and set the angel free.

Your elegance is the angel in your marble. It is your highest potential, the you that will emerge when you start knowing what you want, owning that desire, and asking for it.

In order to advocate, you have to carve away the fear to find that angel. You have to carve away your insecurities, your doubts, and your tendency to try too hard to be like others. The marble is all the things that hide who you really are. It's the stuff that covers up your potential and keeps you from reaching it. You have to do the work of carving away at that marble to be the best advocate you can be. You have to get down to the confident, concentrating angel in the marble. And that angel looks different for everyone.

---

[3]   Mike Power, "Michelangelo's David: I Set It Free," *ARTpublika Magazine* 14 (September 24, 2018).

Carving My Marble

When I started working at the law firm O'Brien and Ryan, I was in law school. Because I had not yet passed the bar, I wasn't allowed to argue in court. I wasn't allowed to question witnesses or take depositions. All I could do was review records, write memos, and do research. But I was lucky, because my mentor was John O'Brien, and he gave me opportunities. He allowed me to come to depositions and trials with him and watch and learn. By the time I graduated from law school and passed the bar, I had a lot of secondhand experience, and I had picked up a lot of John's style. He's an exceptional attorney, and I learned how what he did worked.

Once I'd passed the bar, I had the opportunity to learn under other partners. Dan Ryan is one of the premier medical malpractice defense attorneys in the state of Pennsylvania, if not the country. And I got to learn from him. But his style was different from John's, so I took a piece of that style, too, combining both to create my own. Alan Focht, Dorothy Duffy, Kelly Dunn—each time I had the chance to learn from a new lead on one of my cases, I also seized upon the opportunity to embrace and incorporate a piece of their style, too. I also had the opportunity to watch and learn from their opponents. All of that style stealing was good—until it wasn't. Once I had a little bit of experience under my belt, I realized that by taking on other attorneys' styles, I was adding to the marble.

Looking back, I recognize that before I started adding on more marble, I should have taken the time to find the angel inside me first. I should have been clear on my elegance as an attorney and what I most wanted to be.

Some things I finally understood: I was not a man, and the majority of trial attorneys are men. The things I picked up from them often didn't work for me. Dorothy was cool as a cucumber, and I wasn't. Kelly was tiny and adorable, where I was tall and no one would describe me as adorable. As I continued to try on advocating styles that didn't fit, I got further and further away from my highest potential. My elegance, the angel inside the marble, was getting lost.

When I was prepping for my first trial, I realized I had a problem. I was nervous and scrambling to try and channel one personality or another.

"For this witness I'll be Dan, but for my opening I'll try John. And then for this argument Kelly would do this, and Dorothy would negotiate this way." I felt like I had multiple personalities.

Then the trial started, and I couldn't remember how to be John, Dan, Dorothy, or Kelly. I could barely remember my opening! All I could do was be me—new and naive, driven and determined, and more prepared than anyone else in that courtroom. I won that case, and I realized that finding my own personal advocacy style was going to mean chipping away rather than adding on. I had to recognize who I wanted to be as a trial lawyer and then make choices every day that would support that choice.

I wanted to advocate—with elegance. That would be my style.

It didn't come easy. Trials are combat, so the armor comes up. The armor is my marble. Fear—every day of every trial. Insecurity—almost as often. Doubt, anger (sometimes lots of anger), frustration, and confusion. There was lots of marble to carve away before I found my personal elegance. You have different marble, different fears, and different doubts. But you have your marble, too, and we face a problem Michelangelo didn't face. Our marble grows back, or new marble grows because of a betrayal, an aggression, or a loss. Carving away the marble to find your own personal elegance is a lifelong effort. It isn't one you can outsource. You have to put in the work step by step.

The Moment and the Inner Jury

Part of knowing your elegance and then allowing your Inner Jury to choose things that will support it is what I call *the moment*. It is the moment between what happens to you and what you do in response. In that moment, the Inner Jury goes to work. You Inner Jury determines how you see the situation, your thoughts about the situation, your feelings, and then your actions. She ultimately determines what you get. The key is to capture the moment.

Most of the time when we don't act the way we wish we could, it's because we've missed the moment. Something happens and you react. It's not intentional, not conscious, and often the choice your Inner Jury makes when you react doesn't support your elegance. But if you capture the moment, your action will be a response instead of a reaction. It will be intentional, it will be conscious, and it's far more likely to support your highest potential.

I coach a woman who struggled with this for years. When things happened that made her angry, she "saw red." And then, in her words, she "wasn't responsible for what happened." She'd curse, yell, and be utterly nasty. But she hated it and herself afterwards. She knew that nasty woman wasn't the highest part of her. It wasn't her angel in the marble. She wanted to act in a way that reflected her elegance. But we had to do the work so she would stop reacting and start responding. After months of coaching she was able to manage her anger and she started collecting her wins.

I've had to do that work as well.

One of the toughest and most instructive parts of my courtroom trials was *the moment*, because in trial, I had no choice but to take it. At trial the patient's attorney puts on her case first because the patient has the burden of proof. That means the jury hears the patient's entire case before we get to respond. During that part of the trial, I had to wait. Then, after the patient's attorney asked each one of her witnesses her questions on direct examination, I got to cross-examine that witness. A patient's attorney might have spent two hours on direct examination with her expert, laying out all the ways they claimed my client, the doctor, was negligent and acted below the standard of care. For two hours or more, they would say often horrible, derogatory things about my client. I didn't react. I couldn't react. But during this time my inner voices were often going nuts—seeing things that were wrong, thinking that things weren't fair, and feeling frustrated, angry, and upset. My client was also getting frustrated, and that energy was palpable. The Outer Jury was listening to the other side with rapt attention. But I couldn't do anything other than allow the moment and use it to prepare my response. My Inner Jury had to choose peace and patience. And then, only when opposing counsel was done, I could respond with my questions to challenge that witness's story.

That process was always a forced moment. Initially my Inner Jury would only hear the voices of stress and fear, but as the moment stretched on, my elegance had the chance to take over. The time that passed (between when the expert lied, used misleading words, or hijacked the evidence and the time I stood to ask my questions) was a gift. It gave me time to calm down physically. My body reacted when witnesses lied or misled the jury. I could feel my heartbeat quicken, my face got red and hot. This was a reaction. My body wanted me to jump up, start yelling and spouting my client's story in response.

My mind also reacted—by racing. At first, when the opposing witness started twisting facts and evidence, the voices in my head went crazy.

"That's not true, is it? I need to look at that record again."

"What if I didn't see that in the records? I know I didn't see that, but what if I missed it?"

"I wish John or Dan had tried this case. I'm not ready. I'm not good. Someone else could do this better. I don't want to let my client down. Everyone is watching. I hate this."

If I were allowed to do what I wanted to do in that moment—to react—I'd likely leave. Or I'd scurry around the courtroom looking for each record, whispering vehemently to my associate or paralegal, showing the jury the epitome of confusion. And my Outer Jury would have seen that confusion and felt it themselves. Confusion never wins.

Instead I had no choice but to wait and find mental and physical elegance.

I always waited, and I always captured the moment. I would use the moment to breathe deeply and calm my heartbeat. That helped with the reddening of my face and my body temperature.

Sometimes I'd grab my thumb with the fingers of my opposite hand, using a version of the ancient Japanese art of *Jin Shin* to calm my anxieties. And with that, I was chipping away at my physical manifestations of anxiety. My body found its elegance.

I also used that moment to persuade my Inner Jury to choose calm by looking at the questions I'd planned to ask the witness. I reminded myself that I'd fully prepared, and I knew that to be true. I remembered all the times that I'd recognized that I was the most prepared lawyer in the courtroom and how that had given me the right to believe in myself. Maybe I'd rearrange some of the questions to effectively counter what the expert was saying. Or I might add a new idea, intentionally and with a different colored pen, so that I could follow my train of thought when I stood to face the witness. I gave my Inner Jury choices other than to get upset, and those choices allowed me to chip away at my insecurity, doubt, and confusion to find the elegance inside. My mind found its elegance.

In trials, the moment is guaranteed. The rules say that I can't jump up and react every time the witness says something I don't like. But not every lawyer chooses to follow them and capture that moment. Some lawyers are fun to watch when their opposing witnesses are testifying. They shake their heads, rattle their papers, and sigh. They might object like crazy, popping up and down like a Whack-A-Mole. And when they do get to question the witness they're yelling, flailing, and out of control. Guess what? This is not effective with the Outer Jury. Reactions don't win.

And the same is true for you. Your Inner Jury needs to take a moment in order to remember your elegance—what you want most, your highest potential. She needs to acclimate to what's happening in any given situation. You need to overcome all your biological reactions and make time and space for a response. Slow down. Be willing to be wrong for a moment, so that you can later have a better chance at proving you're right. The more you can respond rather than reacting, the more likely you are to ultimately get what you want. Every time you respond instead of reacting, you're one step closer to your elegance. But you have to choose to capture the moment, and for you it has to be a choice. It won't be forced upon you like it is for me in the courtroom. You have to make the conscious choice to capture the moment. Be aware of your body, your mind, and what they're doing. Practice knowing the difference between reactions and responses. Be conscious of your breathing, how you are seeing the world, and the thoughts that follow. Then be intentional about how you want to respond. Choose your response rather than just letting the reaction happen. That choice will get you closer to your elegance.

Imposters and Aspirers

Sometimes part of choosing your elegance is simply choosing the words you use when you refer to yourself. I have coaching clients who come to me and say, "I have imposter syndrome." We quickly and thoroughly work on that, because neither the premise nor the term will help them become their best selves. They won't reach their elegance thinking that way. The term "imposter syndrome" doesn't serve an advocate. So many of us throw words around without knowing their meaning or how they're impacting us. And "imposter" is a dangerous word.

The definition of *imposter* is "a person who pretends to be someone else to deceive others, especially for fraudulent gain." An imposter is a liar. The only time this term applies to my clients is when they don't know what they really want. If they haven't done the exercises laid out earlier in this chapter and haven't owned their own elegance, they might be pretending. They might be lying, even. But once my clients are clear on what they want and who they want to be, once they're clear on their highest potential, they're no longer lying; they're aspiring. Once you know what you want and who you want to be, you're not lying. You're aspiring. And there is a huge difference.

Aspiring is "directing one's hopes or ambitions toward achieving something." You're aspiring as you direct your hopes and dreams toward your elegance. When you go for that job, ask for that raise, start that business, write that book—you aren't lying; you're aspiring. An imposter is pretending to be something she is not in order to get something. An aspirant is playing the role of something she will be, or perhaps even the role of something she already is but does not know it. She's the angel in the marble, working her way out. Maybe she needs more practice. Maybe she needs more skill. Maybe she needs more people to believe in her ability to be that thing before she can do it. Maybe she needs to believe in herself. No matter what she needs, she will only get it by playing the role of what she will become.

We know the value of this type of play for children. When children play doctor, teacher, pilot, or actress, they're learning valuable skills. Studies show this type of play increases social competence, making children better at social skills, more popular, and better at role-playing.[4] Adults need these same skills, and we get them the same way, by acting, playing, and aspiring. This isn't faking it until you make it, it's showing it until you grow it. And it isn't based on lies. It's based on hopes—aspirations.

Let's stop excusing our inability to achieve our elegance by blaming imposter syndrome and instead embrace aspiration syndrome. It's a much better way to look at such an integral part of growth.

You have one life, one opportunity to achieve your highest potential. Your elegance is there, waiting for you to make the right choices. Everything you aspire to be, every bit of your elegance, is on the other side of fear, doubt, insecurity, and worry. Know what you want and who you want to be, and your Inner Jury can make the choices to get you there.

Precedent

I had a coaching client who ran for political office. Politics, like trial law, is a zero-sum game. Someone wins and someone loses, and that can bring out the worst in people. It brought out the worst in my client's opponent, which brought out the worst in him. When his opponent would go low, he'd follow him to the bottom of the barrel. But he didn't like himself for it.

---

4   Jennifer A. Connolly and Anna-Beth Doyle, "Relation of Social Fantasy Play to Social Competence in Preschoolers," *Developmental Psychology*, 20(5) (1984): 797–806.

He knew what he wanted to be. He wanted to serve his constituents, listen to their challenges, and help them overcome. And he wanted to do it with compassion and purpose. But in moments of stress his Inner Jury kept choosing something else. He got just as dirty as his opponent did.

After some work with me, he decided to give himself more time to respond rather than to react. He decided that he wouldn't respond to his opponent's social media posts, his attack ads, or the rumors he precipitated for twenty-four hours. That twenty-four hours became a nonnegotiable for my client. And once he had that space to respond rather than react, his responses showed his elegance. He'd speak to the issues and not the attack. His opponent wasn't sure what to do with this new routine, and in time he stopped attacking. But it was too late. My client had changed the energy around their interactions and had come closer to his elegance. He won that race, and now we work on maintaining his elegance as he serves his district.

Summary of the Case: Elegance

1. *Your elegance is your highest potential.* The root of the word elegance is "to choose," and you get to choose what you want and who you want to be.
2. *The moment between what happens and your response is magic.* When you choose to respond rather than

react, you give your Inner Jury the chance to make the choice that serves your elegance.

3. *You are not an imposter.* Once you know what you want, you're no longer lying. You're just practicing becoming your highest potential. You're trying your elegance on for size.

Chapter 2
Words

You create as you speak.

Words are powerful.

Every single word you use matters. You're choosing every word, whether with intention or without. The words you choose when you're speaking to yourself and your Inner Jury change the decisions you make. And that could change your entire life. The words you choose when you are speaking to your Outer Jury, the people you want to influence and persuade, change the way they see the world.

Words are magic.

Lawyers use words to win. We twist them, choose them, and play with them. We use them as weapons and as treats. If you want to advocate for yourself and your dreams you have to do the same. First, you have to accept that every word matters. Every word you use helps to make sure that your message resonates with your jury. Facts tell, stories sell, but advocates win. One of the reasons advocates win is because they choose their words well.

Words are armor.

During my trials, the most stressful part for me was when my client, usually a doctor, was on the stand and being cross-examined. At that point she was advocating for herself. I'd provided her with the armor to protect her from the attack. I'd armed her with evidence, credibility, presentation, and reception. And I'd *begged* her to memorize her own deposition.

"Your deposition contains your words. And if you contradict yourself, you lose huge amounts of credibility. So, memorize that deposition. Know all the words, because every word matters."

By the time my client was being cross-examined she had acquired the tools to win, but she still had to *use them*. She had to answer the questions, counter the attack, build her credibility, and convince the jury. How? She did it all with words. My job during cross was to object when the questions were improper. We both had our roles, and they both involved words.

In one trial, my client was being cross-examined about pedal pulses, the pulses that doctors feel in your feet. Before patients have surgery on their legs, doctors often feel these pulses to see if the legs have enough blood flow to safely have the surgery. In this case the patient had pedal pulses the doctor could feel (palpable pedal pulses—a tongue twister that the jury enjoyed watching the attorneys try to master). But after the surgery the patient's feet lost blood flow and she had to have both feet amputated. The patient's attorney said the doctor should have done more tests on her blood flow before the surgery. He said that feeling the pedal pulses wasn't enough. My doctor and my expert said that feeling the pulses was enough. They were going to testify that feeling the pedal pulses was the standard of care, the thing doctors were trained to do in that situation.

During my doctor's cross-examination, the patient's attorney made a big show of taking out my doctor's deposition and "reading" from the transcript. Depositions are where attorneys have the opportunity to question witnesses before trial in order to get the information they need to ask different kinds of questions at trial. And this attorney was referring to the page where my doctor had agreed that, in an ideal world, they'd test every patient's blood flow with specific equipment called a Doppler. But in the deposition my client also explained that doctors don't use the Doppler on every patient because there isn't the time or the equipment or the staffing or the evidence that it prevents harm.

The opposing attorney didn't want the jury to hear all that. Instead he asked, "Doctor, didn't you tell me in your deposition that you should have used the Doppler?"

Those words were, indeed, damning.

If the doctor had actually said that, we might have talked about settling the case. And if the jury believed that the doctor had said that, we might have lost the case. But that's not what the doctor had said in his deposition. He said, "In an ideal world we would measure every patient's Dopplers." The attorney was changing the doctor's words while trying to suggest that he was reading directly from the deposition, all in an effort to mislead the jury. He was twisting the words, and words matter. I yearned to jump up and yell, "Objection, Your Honor! Words matter!"

But that's not the way trials work. I would have my turn. My doctor had his armor. We'd prepared for this. And I had to trust that he had the tools to advocate for himself.

"Could you show me on what page of my deposition I said that? Because I believe what I said was that in an ideal world that would happen, but that there are numerous reasons why that didn't make sense for the patient."

The doctor knew every word of his deposition. He knew it wasn't enough to remember the gist of his deposition or the theme of what he'd said. He knew that every word had power and meaning.

Every word mattered.

The attorney tried to move on to the next question. The doctor said, "I'm glad to answer that question, but first could you show me where in my deposition I said that?"

"Doctor, I'm the one asking the questions," the lawyer said, with a red face. His words were coming back to haunt him.

That was the moment we won that case. Credibility is paramount at trial, and the attorney who had tried to mislead the jury lost his credibility in that moment. If they couldn't believe that the deposition said what he told them it said, what could they believe? My doctor had known the words he used, what they meant, and why he used them.

He'd used the words to advocate. That's how you use your armor.

Using Words with Your Inner Jury

"Abracadabra!"

You've heard that word?

Magicians use it before they pull a rabbit out of a hat or make someone disappear. They use it to create magic. But do you know what the word means? It is an Aramaic phrase that means

"I will create as I speak." That's how you make magic. You create as you speak.

What are you creating in your body, in your mind, and in your spirit when you speak to yourself? If you're using negative, derogatory, or defeatist words, you're not creating an advocate. You're creating negativity and defeat. In order to advocate for yourself to the Outer Jury, the Inner Jury has to believe. If you want to create self-confidence, strength, elegance, and an effective advocate, you want the words you choose to use with yourself and your Inner Jury to reflect it.

The words you use impact your confidence. When you speak to yourself nicely, you're bound to feel nice about yourself. When you give yourself the gift of praise, you start to shine. Some people even believe that the words you use when talking to yourself can impact your health as well. Dr. Masaru Emoto was a Japanese author famous for his water experiments. His published work *Messages from Water and the Universe* contains experiments with words and photographs of ice crystals.[5] He'd put water in different containers and speak to each container differently. With some he'd use kind, supportive, and loving words, and with others he'd use hateful, negative words. The water that he'd spoken to with loving words contained beautiful crystals under the microscope, while the water that he'd spoken to with hateful words was ugly under the microscope. If up to 60 percent of the human body is water, are you running on mostly mud or mostly crystals?

Canadian author Danielle LaPorte followed up Emoto's water experiment with an experiment done on Instagram and dubbed

---

[5]   Masaru Emoto, *Messages from Water and the Universe* (Carlsbad, CA: Hay House, 2010).

#theappleexperiment. She encouraged people to cut an apple in half and put half in a jar and speak to it with positive, loving words. The other half went in another jar, where people spoke to it in hateful words. The pictures of the apples on social media appear to show that the apple that received the loving words was less rotten, brown, and shriveled. Words impact reality.

The words we use also influence how we see things. One of my favorite examples involves keys, and it helps to remind me that words are the key to advocating. In the French language the word *key* is feminine, and in the German language the word *key* is masculine. Researchers asked native French speakers who had lived in the United States and spoke fluent English to describe keys. They also asked native German speakers who had lived in the United States for years and spoke fluent English to describe keys. The French described keys as tiny, delicate, and intricate. The Germans described them as heavy and strong.[6] The words they used influenced the way they saw the keys. Words influence the way you see the world as well.

The words you use create pathways. If you look at a path in the woods or in the snow, it's created by repetition. People have walked that same way over and over until it has created a path for others to follow. Recent research on the neuroplasticity of the brain tells us that our neural pathways are the same. Our brains create actual physical paths when we act the same say, do the same things, or speak the same words. Those become our neural pathways, and in time they determine who we are. When you

---

[6]   Lera Boroditsky and Lauren A. Schmidt, "Sex, Syntax, and Semantics," *Proceedings of the Annual Meeting of the Cognitive Science Society*, 22 (2000); retrieved from https://escholarship.org/uc/item/0tj9w8zf.

want to influence and persuade your Inner Jury, you have to be intentional about the words you use and the pathways you create.

You have to know what words mean—what is the definition of the ones you're using—and be aware of how you're using them in your inner self talk. Once you're keenly aware of the words you're choosing in talking to yourself, you can more carefully use them to advocate.

One of my jobs as a coach is to help my clients choose words that serve them. Most of the time my clients don't even see that they're choosing words that hurt their chances for success. But when I point it out to them, they suddenly become more and more aware of just how often they choose words without thinking. Then we work together to find another choice, try it on for size, and see whether that word gets them closer to their elegance.

Using Words to Advocate Your Outer Jury

The words you use can determine whether or not your Outer Jury will believe you. Credibility is one of the tools of an advocate. You want your Outer Jury to believe you. And if you don't choose carefully, your words can get in the way.

Often when I tell people I was a trial attorney for more than twenty years they ask me whether I'm especially good at identifying when someone is lying. I am. I can do it by reading body language and listening to tone of voice. Once you learn about Presentation and Reception you'll likely find yourself better at that as well. But one of the easiest ways to suspect that someone is lying is by their word choice. When people choose to use the passive voice, they're often lying.

Imagine you're questioning a colleague about why he scheduled a meeting without including you.

"I was told you didn't want to come."

That's the passive voice—and I'd immediately have my suspicions about whether that was true. I can't verify this statement. He hasn't given me a person to check with to see whether it's true. There's no one else for me to question, no one to corroborate his story.

On the other hand, if he had said, "Sally said you didn't want to come," I would be far more likely to believe him. Because either he's telling the truth or Sally is in on the lie. Either way, there's further discovery to be had because there's a way to validate the story. And simply by using the right words, he has built credibility with me.

Whether you're the speaker or the listener, watch for the passive voice. When you choose those words, you might be losing precious credibility with your listener. And when you hear those words, your antenna for lies should be tingling. Words matter.

Words also matter when you're asking questions. One of the most popular chapters in my first book, *The Elegant Warrior: How to Win Life's Trials Without Losing Yourself,* is the chapter on curiosity (Chapter 3). In that chapter, I tell a story about Judge Rosemarie Aquilina, who was the judge in the Larry Nassar case. Larry Nassar was a physician at Michigan State University accused of molesting hundreds of young female gymnasts. In January 2018, Judge Aquilina presided over a sentencing hearing for Nassar and allowed the victims to speak (over the objections of Nassar's attorneys). Judge Aquilina is famous for the way she empowered the women who came forward to testify against him. In that chapter, I posit that her ability to give the women so much power was found in her choice of words. As each woman came forward, she didn't say, "What do I need to know?" She didn't say, "Tell me what happened." She said, "Tell me what you want me to know." I believe that choice of words changed everything, in that courtroom and beyond. Many readers of *The Elegant Warrior* have told me they've chosen those words, or similar ones, and changed their relationships as well.

Judge Aquilina is, like me, very conscious of the words she chooses. She, too, understands the power of words. We've become friends, and while writing this book I was talking to her about words as a tool of an advocate. Once again, she easily and quickly shared some wisdom I won't soon forget.

"I don't think anyone should use the word *why*."

My mind started spinning and, to be honest, objecting. I didn't agree. Questions are one of the tools of an advocate, and we all know that questions begin with "who, what, when, where, and why."

"What do you mean?" I asked. "Why don't you like *why*?"

And with that question I'd proven her point. Judge Aquilina feels that the word *why* puts people on the defense. Judge Aquilina sees the impact of this word firsthand in some of her more difficult cases. When she presides over sexual assault cases, far too often she sees the impact of asking "why."

"Why didn't you call for help?"

"Why were you out alone?"

"Why were you wearing that skirt?"

It's no wonder she's not a fan of *why*. Judge Aquilina feels that the word is fine for scientific endeavors, but she feels it has no place in personal relationships. She told me that when she uses the word with her children it shuts down communication, but when she chooses other words the entire conversation changes.

Since that conversation I find, when I use the word *why*, I question myself. I thought I knew what *why* meant, but I wanted to be sure. I looked it up. It means "for what cause, reason, or purpose." And that's why it can put people on the defense. When you're looking for a cause or a reason, it's often that you're searching for something negative. It's often to find something or someone to blame. Why did you get sick? Why did you lose money? Why did you gain weight? *Why* is often used to explore reasons for negative things, and we use a different word to explain positive things.

We say, "Why did you get sick?" We don't say, "Why did you get well?" Instead we say, "How did you get well?" We look for one thing to blame when things are negative but look for a process to follow when things are good.

We say, "Why did you lose money?" We don't say, "Why did you make money?" We say, "How did you make money?" Again, we're not using words to blame but rather to understand.

And we say, "Why did you gain weight?" but not often "Why did you lose weight?" More often we say, "How did you lose weight?"

When we use the word *why* we're often looking for someone or someone to blame. And even if we're not, the person on the other end of the word is likely to feel defensive. Words can make people feel a certain way, even if that's not our intent when we speak. Judge Aquilina made me more conscious of how and when I use the word *why*.

All this doesn't mean we should never say *why*. As advocates, there are going to be times that we want to make someone feel defensive. When you've caught someone in a lie, when they've hurt you and you want them to feel bad about it, *why* may be your best choice. And when you're resorting to the last tool of an advocate, Argument, you often want the other person to feel defensive. During argument, Questions can be used to teach but also to challenge, to support but also to slay. Choose your *why* carefully. Make your words work for you.

Breaking the Curse

Once you're clear on the words you want to use, you have to make sure that your Outer Jury understands those words. Often they don't. We forget that people don't know what we know. This has been described as the *curse of knowledge*,[7] and a big part of my work with my clients is helping them to break that curse, which can be deadly.

When I think of one of the first cases in my career, the stairs of one man's home are what I most remember. One afternoon I stood at the bottom of these steep, dark, and narrow stairs at a rowhome in Philadelphia, and I dreaded the climb. I was in my pinstripe suit, with my hair in the ponytail that signified I was stepping into my attorney role. But I didn't feel sure or confident. I knew when I reached the top of those stairs I'd step into a dying man's home. That man had sued my doctor, claiming that he'd failed to diagnose the cancer that was now killing him. My job was to climb those stairs and take his deposition, asking him questions about his pain, his anger, his regrets, and his death.

---

[7]   Chip Heath and Dan Heath, "The Curse of Knowledge," *Harvard Business Review* (December 2006).

But that wasn't all. I knew that when I reached the top of those stairs, I'd also have to challenge him.

I'd spoken to my experts about the case. While the patient and his attorney claimed my doctor had failed to diagnose his cancer, my client and my experts had a different story. They said that the doctor had made the appropriate recommendation. The doctor had recommended that the patient have an MRI. He'd made that recommendation in the patient portal, the place where the doctor and patient would communicate online. The patient had never had that MRI, and my experts said that if he had gone for the MRI as recommended the cancer likely would have been diagnosed. I had to climb those stairs and place some of the blame for the reason I was there on the patient himself.

As I approached the top of the stairs, I could smell the distinctive odor of a hospital room and I could hear the beeps and pings of the machines that kept the man alive. When I reached the top, I stepped directly into the man's small home. There he sat in a hospital bed that took up the entirety of the room. The court reporter who would take down everything we said was seated at the head of the bed on a turned-over trash can because there was no room for a chair. The patient's attorney was at the other side of the head of the bed, so I approached the foot of the bed with my notebook and my trepidation at the ready.

I asked him questions. I asked him about his love, his life, and his work. I asked him about his pain, his losses, and his regrets. And finally, I had to ask the question that was so important in this case.

"Sir, why didn't you have the MRI that the doctor recommended?"

His answer? "I didn't know what an MRI was."

"I'd already had X-rays, CAT scans, and so many tests. I didn't want another one. I didn't want to pay another co-pay or take the bus to the hospital another time."

My mind was reeling. "Sir, why didn't you ask what an MRI was?"

He grimaced. "I was embarrassed. I didn't know who was reading what I wrote in the patient portal, and I didn't want people to know I didn't know what it was."

In that case, the curse of knowledge really was a curse. The doctor had the curse of knowledge—he knew what an MRI was, and he knew it so well he forgot what it was like not to know it. He used a word (actually, an acronym) that his "jury" didn't understand. And it was a deadly choice. As a result, I had to climb those stairs and take that deposition. As a result, that man died two weeks later.

We settled that case, but not until after he'd passed away. My greatest regret about that case is that the patient never knew what an impact he'd had on the doctor. Because the doctor learned that he had the curse of knowledge, and he worked every day to overcome it. He asked more questions and used the phone for important conversations rather than the patient portal. The doctor realized that every word mattered, and he became a better advocate for himself, his care plans, and his patients as a result.

You have the curse of knowledge as well. It might be that you have the curse when it comes to your area of expertise. I coach tech professionals who have the curse when it comes to coding, and I work with real estate professionals who have the curse when it comes to accelerated cost recovery systems. Some clients have the curse when it comes to their wants, their needs, or their pain. Others don't have *your* knowledge or *your* experience. When you remember and acknowledge that, you can use your words to break the curse and build understanding.

Words Matter

An advocate uses words to create connections, change perspectives, and change lives. You can't get what you want until you ask for it, and you have to ask for it with words that will make you most likely to get it.

Here are some ways to make sure you're choosing your words well.

1. *When you're advocating in writing, read your words out loud.* We write more formally than we speak, and so the curse of knowledge is going to rear its ugly head much more when your message is written. By reading your message out loud, you can make sure the words you use will be received in a way that works. Read your message to someone else to test the impact of your words. Ask them what the words make them think, feel, or want to do. Test the impact of your words before you use them.

2. *Know what words mean.* Far too often we assume we know what something means. I've stopped assuming. I look up words all the time. In fact, when I'm reading on my Kindle I look up words so often that the Kindle recently popped up with an icon asking if I wanted a simpler version of the book I was reading! I don't want a simple version. I want to be sure I'm understanding the

version in front of me. In order to understand the book, I have to understand the words. And in order to advocate, I need to choose the words that best communicate my message. You do, too. Look words up as soon as you read or hear them if you can. If you can't right at the time, make a list and look them up later. Understand the words that you use so that you can help others to understand your message and get what you're advocating for.

3. *Play with words.* Since I believe words have magical powers, I like to play with them. This means I don't just look up the definitions of the words I want to use. I also look up where the words come from—their origin. When I looked up the root of the word *elegance* and found it is "to choose," I was able to see the word differently. Elegance is a choice, and you can choose your highest potential. Now I remind people that they choose their elegance and encourage them to make it an intentional choice. Knowing that has made the word even more important, powerful, and useful for me, and for other words as well. Look up a word root or search its meaning. Start with your name. You might find meaning there that could give you a power you didn't know you had.

4. *Use your thesaurus.* I love to look up word synonyms. When you're advocating for yourself and your ideas, you want to do the same. If you know one hundred ways to say a thing, you are far more likely to be able to choose the best way to say it to your jury. You can choose the way that is most likely to resonate with the people you want to persuade.

Sometimes that means picking the simplest word, sometimes the prettiest, sometimes the most scientific, and sometimes the most powerful. You might not be aware of all the choices that are available to you. Make yourself aware and then choose with intention.

5. *Read.* The more you read, the more likely you are to come across words that you've never seen before. Seeing words is different than hearing them. Both have their value, but when you see a word, you are more likely to see its magic. And when you're reading you get to see the word in context and try to figure it out on your own. The words around it give you clues, and punctuation is also a guide. For me reading is more than learning about the topic of the book. It's also learning about words and how I can use them. Every word I learn is a weapon in my arsenal. You can't be an Elegant Warrior without your words.

Words change things. They change us, and they change our potential.

Precedent

I love helping my clients choose new words (almost as much as I love helping them choose new perspectives). I had one client whose choice of words changed her life. She's a phenomenal leader, but the pandemic and its fallout knocked her for a loop. A number of her team members resigned at once, and she was frustrated, confused, and angry. Her first thought was *I failed*.

I asked her to question that story. How could she see things differently? She pondered it for a moment, and then had a different story. "They (the people who resigned) failed." I understood how that felt better to her. If you blame someone else, it often feels better. But I asked her to question the idea of failure. What other words could we use instead?

Ultimately, she agreed that even failure was a discovery. She decided to try that word on for size. "I discovered." Every time she failed, she discovered what didn't work. Ideally, she also discovered what did. She discovered that the old ways of leading wouldn't work in the current environment. And her team discovered that they may have jumped out of a frying pan and into a fire. But those discoveries could serve her as a leader (and the team members who came asking for their jobs back later).

Words matter. Choose the words that feel best and allow you to be your best.

Summary of the Case: Words

1. *When you speak to yourself, use words that help you grow.* If words can change water and apples, they can certainly change you.
2. *When addressing your Outer Jury, use words as tools.* Familiarize yourself with them and play with them.

Just like you wouldn't use a wrench to hammer a nail, the wrong word will never get the job done.

3. *One word can mean the difference between a win and a loss.* Whether we're talking about lost cases, lost opportunities, or lost potential, don't let your words be your downfall.

Chapter 3

Perspective

Choose what you see, change what you get.

Early in my career as a keynote speaker, I had an activity I'd do with my audience. It was designed to show them the power of perspective.

In the activity I'd give everyone in the room a piece of paper, a rubber band, and a golf pencil without an eraser. I'd hold up the paper.

"This is a piece of paper."

I'd hold up the pencil.

"This is a pencil."

And then I'd hold up the rubber band.

"This could be a rubber band."

Then I'd ask them to write their initials on the paper with the pencil.

"Erase it."

People would usually look at me in confusion. Some would look around to see if other people had erasers. Others would wet their finger and see if they could wipe the writing clean. But a few would take some time to play. They'd play with other perspectives, other ways of seeing the rubber band. And in that play, they'd figure out that a rubber band could also be an eraser. And that was the point—change the way you look at things and the things you look at change. That's the power of perspective.

I chose this activity after reading about it. Scientists conducted an experiment—that actual experiment is where I got the idea for this exercise. In the experiment, the researchers told some people, "This is a rubber band." They told other people, "This could be a rubber band." Only 3 percent of the people told "this is" a rubber band realized it could be used as an eraser. But 40 percent of those told it "could be" a rubber band saw they could use it to erase their mistake.[8] The words "could be" completely changed a person's perspective.

Perspective is defined as "a way of regarding something," and the root is "to look at through." Perspective is looking at something through a specific lens, but the lens can change. One of the greatest gifts I received from my work as a trial attorney was an ability to see the truth differently. I bet you think there's one "truth" out there. But I know that most of the time, there isn't. In my trials, the patient and her attorney had one version of the truth. In their version, the doctor made a mistake. Sometimes, in their version, the doctor is a liar. Sometimes she's operating for money; other times she's letting a junior doctor perform too much of the operation. Their truth includes a doctor who made a mistake, which caused the patient's injury. Often that truth is

---

[8]   Ellen J. Langer and Alison I. Piper, "The Prevention of Mindlessness," *Journal of Personality and Social Psychology*, 53(2) (1987): 280–287.

what the patient has to believe in order to fuel the fire of anger. Without it, nothing would make sense.

My client and I always had another version of the truth. Our version was sometimes some iteration of *bad stuff happens.* Bad things happen to people, and it doesn't have to be anyone's fault. But other times, in our version of the truth, it was the patient who made a mistake. She didn't follow directions or come to the doctor soon enough. He didn't do what the doctor recommended. Sometimes our version included blaming another doctor or another circumstance. And often our truth was what the doctor has to believe in order to keep going to work. Without it, every day could be the day they hurt another patient. No doctor goes to work for that.

Every witness who testified in my trials either took an oath to tell the truth or affirmed that he would. And I believed when each witness testified he was certain he was telling the truth. But that means there are as many truths as there are witnesses, because every story differs a little. Some stories are completely contradictory. It was my job to take the other side's story and help the jury see things through my perspective.

Ultimately, the jury determines the truth. The jurors listen to the patient's truth and the doctor's truth. Then they go into the jury deliberation room, decide which perspective they believe (that's why credibility is so important), and come out to declare what is true. But that's just their version of the truth—their agreed-upon perspective. The jury has decided how they will see things.

An advocate's job is to change the jury's lens so that they see what you want them to see, because sight leads to thoughts, which leads to emotions, then action, then reaction/response/result.

That's how we steer (STEER) our lives.

- Sight
- Thought
- Emotion
- Enaction
- Reaction/Response/Result

That makes perspective a powerful tool when you advocate to win.

What You See Is What You Get

When I say, "What you see is what you get," I mean it very literally. What you see truly is what you get. When you see the world as a dangerous place, you often get danger. When you see people as mean and nasty, you often get mean and nasty. And, on the other hand, when you see the world as an abundant place, you get abundance, and when you see people as kind, you get kindness.

Motivational speaker and author Dr. Wayne Dyer has been one of my greatest teachers. I've read all his books and listened to most of his teachings. In one of them, he told a version of the following story, which illustrates this idea that what you see is what you get. He was walking down the beach near his home in beautiful Hawaii when a woman approached him. She told him she was thinking of moving to Hawaii and asked him if she'd like it.

"How do you like where you live now?"

"Oh, I hate it. The people are nasty, the weather is bad, and the streets are dirty. Everyone is annoying, and I just can't wait to get out of there."

Wayne told her, "Oh, I think you'll find it much the same here." He knew that the way she saw the world impacted what she got.

Later he passed another woman who also approached.

"I'm thinking of moving to Hawaii, and I wonder if you'd tell me how you think I'd like it."

"Well, how do you like it where you live now?"

"I love it. The people are just lovely, kind, and friendly. The weather is usually good, and even when it rains there's something special about it. The streets are bustling with fun. I'm sad to leave, but I'm eager for a new experience."

"Oh, I think you'll find it much the same here."

What you see is what you get. If you see the world as lovely, friendly, and fun, you'll get more love, friends, and fun. When you see the world as angry, scared, and boring, you'll get angry, scared, and bored. *What you see is what you get.*

Fortunately, you can change what you see, and you can change what others see as well. If the jury sees my doctor as someone who doesn't care, who is just looking to make a buck or who rushes through surgery, that's a problem. If they see her as compassionate, kind, and patient, then that's a problem for the other side. Sometimes you have to change what your Outer Jury sees in order to win. In the courtroom it was my job to change what the jury saw. When the jurors first see the parties in the case, they often see a patient who looks a lot like them. Every one of my jurors is a patient. In fact, everyone in the courtroom, including the doctor, is a patient. But not one of my jurors has ever been a doctor. Not one of my jurors walks into the courtroom seeing life, or the case, through the doctor's perspective. My job was to help them and, more importantly, to teach my witnesses to do the same.

Remember, facts tell, stories sell, but advocates win. In the courtroom there are plenty of facts to be had, but ultimately there are two stories the jury will hear. They have to choose which perspective is true. Most of the time, truth is a matter of perspective.

You have your juries, and they have their perspectives. Your clients see the world through a specific lens. Your teammates, your investors, your customers, your partners, and your families all have their perspectives. You see opportunity and they see risk. You see blame and they see reason. When you're advocating for something you want, you often have to change what they see. Remember, what you see is what you get. Change what they see, change what they get—and change what you get as well.

This starts with your Inner Jury. Before you can change what the Outer Jury sees, you have to change what your Inner Jury sees. If you can change your own perspective, it's much easier to change that of others.

The Inner Jury is the part of you that decides what you see, think, and feel. It decides what you'll do and who you'll be. It's always choosing between the stories you tell yourself. It's choosing between perspectives. One might be that you can't do what you want to do or be what you want to be. Another is that you should quit, give up, or hide. If you believe those perspectives, they can and do stop you long before anyone else gets a chance. But there's always another perspective for the Inner Jury to choose. You could choose to see things differently—that you can do, or be, anything. When we change what we see, we change what we think, what we feel, how we act, and what we get. That's so rewarding that you'll want to employ this tactic over and over as you work on using the perspective tool to change minds.

Changing Your Own Perspective

What's your perspective?

Sometimes it's hard to recognize that you are seeing the world through a specific lens. Fish don't know that they're looking through water. It's all they know. That's just their worldview. And you might not realize that you're looking through the lens of your genes, your gender, or your ethnicity. You might not see that you're swimming in your training, your culture, and your expectations.

Before you can change your perspective, you have to realize that you have one.

My weight loss was the result of a change in perspective. When I was young I was a little chubby. I'd rather read than play outside, and I'd rather eat candy and chips than fish and broccoli. I saw candy and ice cream as a treat. When I got a little older I started seeing my body from a perspective that hurt me. I saw myself as unathletic, unattractive, and unwieldy. I dieted. I saw diets as a way of punishing myself for having a body I didn't love. I saw restriction as punishment for not being what I wanted to be. All that I saw led to thoughts of dislike for my body, thoughts of attachment to food, and thoughts of failure over the next doomed diet. That, of course, led to actions of restriction and then excess. I started to see my body as an enemy I had to control, and what I saw was what I got.

Then, very suddenly, I chose a different perspective.

I remember the day it happened. I was a freshman in college at American University. I'd recently called my mother crying because Zeke, an upperclassman I'd had a crush on, had called me fat. He didn't know I'd heard him and he said it in an off-hand way, but it stung, and it only affirmed the way I already saw myself.

My poor mother didn't know what to say or do. She tried to comfort me on the call, but there was no comfort to be had. But about two weeks later, when I asked her for money to join the gym at school, she found the perfect words. She sent me a card with a check in it. The front of the card said, "When I sit across the porch from God, I'll thank Him for sending me you."

Inside she wrote me a message. She didn't write about my weight or diets or even our conversation about Zeke. Instead she wrote about how she saw me. She told me I was beautiful, strong, and fun. She reminded me of my kindness, compassion, and inner light. Then she ended the note with this.

"Here's the money that you need to join the gym. But don't do it to be anything different than what you are. Do it to be stronger, inside and out. Do it to move the way you want to move. Join the gym, if you want, but do it to be healthy and to treat yourself with love." She allowed me to see joining the gym as a way to choose my elegance. Suddenly, there was another voice and another perspective for my Inner Jury to consider.

I saw things differently. I saw the gym as a place to get more confidence, more flexibility, and more of a glow. I saw eating well as a way to feel better, move better, and shine. My Inner

Jury had to choose what to see, and I chose to see this new perspective. That led to new thoughts. No longer was I in a rush to get to a certain weight or a certain size. Instead, every day was a step closer to glowing more. Those thoughts led to feelings of excitement rather than resignation, and the new action was that I worked out far more and ate far less. When I chose to see my body in a new way, I got a new body.

When I chose the way I saw my body, I changed my entire life.

I've since consistently worked at choosing what I see when I want to change what I get. I think being a trial attorney made this so much easier. I'm trained and experienced in seeing all sides of an issue. I have to see my doctor's side, obviously. But I also have to see the other side's case just as clearly so I can defend against it. And I don't stop there. I try to imagine the jurors' perspectives, the judge's perspective, and the doctor's perspective. When I can see things many ways, I can see many ways to win.

It's also served me in my work on television. I started doing legal analysis for CNN, Fox News Channel, MSNBC, and NBC in 2013. Most of the time when a producer called, they wanted me to take a side in the latest legal argument of the day. Some attorneys refused to take the side they didn't agree with, but I was open to seeing things from either side and making an argument to support what I saw. It's a lawyer's job, after all. But some people can't even imagine being able to see both sides of an argument. I've received plenty of nasty emails, tweets, and messages about the arguments I've made on television. Every time I read one of those messages I think to myself, "I bet this person isn't very good at getting what he wants."

Here are three ways you can get better at seeing things from a different perspective:

1. *Use your imagination.* Every time you're faced with a situation, a choice, a decision, or any inner turmoil, consider how many different ways you can see the situation. Consider it from the perspective of everyone it touches. That means not just the main players (you and your ex, fighting over childcare) but also your children, your in-laws, your nanny, your best friend who listens to your complaints time after time. If you constantly ask yourself, "What view am I missing?" you'll get much better at seeing them all. Once you choose a different Sight, you can choose a different Thought, which leads to a different Emotion. Enaction and Reaction then follow. You can STEER your way to a different goal.

2. *Rose/Bud/Thorn.* When I work one-on-one coaching clients, I give them exercises to help them switch perspectives. One of those exercises is the Rose/Bud/Thorn exercise. I ask them to take a specific situation (being fired, the fight they just had with their partner, a fender bender they had on the way to work) and find the rose, the bud, and the thorn in that specific situation. (Meaning, the beauty, the potential, and the downside.) It has to be specific. Sometimes my clients get lazy and want to use, "Well, I didn't die," as their rose in what looks to be a bad situation. That doesn't help because the work done in finding the rose is what will help you get better at seeing other perspectives. Here's a personal example from my life in the COVID-19 pandemic. I was writing this book in the midst of it and had been under a stay-at-home order in New York City for fifty days. I easily found

thorns—I missed touching another human, going on dates, seeing my parents; I lost five keynotes. The thorns went on and on. And I could see the buds—this book was completed before things got back to "normal." I also created my first online course with those tools. Finding the rose was harder. It was tempting to slip into, "Well, I didn't get sick," and that's the consistent rose. When you have your health, there's always a rose. However, with some work I was able to go deeper. My new rose is clarity. I found some clarity about what I wanted to do with this book, my course, and my business going forward. I'm much clearer that the rest of my life is going to be focused on teaching others to advocate for themselves because I see that they'll need it more than ever. That clarity is a rose.

3. *Work backward.* When you can't see how what you see is impacting a situation, work with the other factors.

    Sight
    Thought
    Emotion
    Enaction
    Reaction/Response/Result

    If you're discouraged because you didn't get the job you interviewed for, start there. That's emotion. You're discouraged. What is the thought that is making you feel that way?

"I'll never get another interview."

"That was the job I was meant to have."

"I don't have the qualifications I need to succeed."

Now consider what is leading you to have those thoughts. What do you see, and how could you see things differently? If you see the job market as limited, the thought makes sense. If you see it as abundant, all of a sudden the thought changes. If you see this job as a perfect unicorn, the thought makes sense, but if you choose to see a world where that job could have led to late nights, stressful days, and thankless hours of work, new emotion. If you see your resume as simply a list of skills, it might make sense to question your qualifications, but if you see the story of how those skills transfer to the job you want, suddenly you've got a new thought.

You can start anywhere in the process and work your way back to what you see. But your perspective is always where it begins. Once you master changing your own perspective you can move on to changing that of other people. This process is influenced by life coach Brooke Castillo's work. She is one of my greatest mentors, and the model that she developed is the basis for this STEER method. It is also the model I use with many of my coaching clients.

Changing Others' Perspectives

You have no authority with people you don't understand.

When you're willing and able to see things from other people's perspective, things get a whole lot easier. I saw that in a trial I had with a woman named Mrs. Hernandez. Mrs. Hernandez sued my client, the doctor, after she had surgery on her shoulder and sustained a nerve injury. Her claim was that the doctor had made a mistake during the surgery. Our defense was that this type of nerve injury was a recognized risk of this surgery, and it could happen in the absence of negligence. It was basically the *stuff happens* defense, which is not my favorite but often the truth. Before every case goes to trial, I first talk to the doctor and the insurance company about settlement. Even when, as was the case with Mrs. Hernandez, the doctor had done everything right, settlement sometimes makes sense. For example, in those situations where the jury is going to have a very difficult time seeing past their sympathy, or seeing things from a medical perspective, the risk of losing makes settlement more attractive. Other times the doctor sees the trial as a huge source of stress and risk, and she'd rather settle if we can. Perspectives play a huge role in making settlement determinations.

But my doctor, my insurance rep, and I all agreed on the approach we were going to take with this case. We were going to trial to try to influence the jury to see and believe our perspective.

The trial was a little unusual because Mrs. Hernandez didn't speak English. That meant she had to have a translator at the trial. Every day I'd be the first to arrive in the courtroom, and soon thereafter Mrs. Hernandez would come in with her translator. I knew from the answers she'd given at her deposition that Mrs. Hernandez didn't have any family in the US. Her daughter and her husband had both died, and the rest of her family still lived in Cuba. I also knew that she didn't leave the house much but instead liked to stay home and watch TV.

The trial lasted two weeks, and when it was done the jury could not reach a verdict. In my cases ten of the twelve jurors have to agree on a verdict, and they couldn't. That meant they were hung. We lawyers had the opportunity to talk to them after and found out that seven had seen the case my way and five had seen the case the patient's way. That meant we'd have to try the case again, but it also meant that we both still had risk. Neither side had a slam dunk, so it made sense to explore a settlement. During a pretrial conference with the judge in preparation for the second trial, I made an offer.

Mrs. Hernandez's attorney liked the offer. One of the tools of an advocate is Reception, and I could tell by the way he leaned in and smiled, and by his tone of voice that he would take it if he could. But it wasn't his decision. He took the offer to Mrs. Hernandez, communicating it to her through the translator. And she said no. She didn't counter; she didn't explain. Just no. Her attorney was clearly frustrated, and he asked the judge to speak to her. The judge explained the offer and the risk she was taking by rejecting it to Mrs. Hernandez through her translator. Again, she said, "no." She didn't counter, and she didn't blink. It didn't make sense to any of us because we weren't seeing the trial through her perspective.

We had to try the case again.

This time I watched Mrs. Hernandez even more closely. Every morning as she walked into the courtroom with her translator, she grinned. At lunch time she'd go out with her translator and sometimes her attorney. She'd attempt to start conversation with me during breaks, and though we were limited by our language differences she beamed with pleasure at the attempt. That's when it hit me: Mrs. Hernandez saw the trial as fun. While the doctor and I saw the case as stressful, risky, and intense, she saw it as an opportunity to get out of her house, interact with people, speak her native language, and watch the drama of a trial unfold. Her perspective was unusual but understandable. Her perspective meant that it would have been almost impossible to have settled the case.

We could have tried. If we'd known Mrs. Hernandez's perspective, we could have attempted a creative settlement. Maybe it would include regular visits with a translator or someone who spoke her language. We could have explored using some of the settlement monies to get her into a community program or group. There were things, other than money, that would have impacted the way Mrs. Hernandez saw a settlement offer, but we didn't even try because we didn't see her perspective.

When the second trial was over, the jury took less than two hours to come to a verdict. While we stood in the courtroom, waiting for the foreperson to announce it, I looked over at Mrs. Hernandez and she looked like the cat who ate the canary. Even when the foreperson announced that the jury had found for my client and she'd lost, her smile never wavered. Perhaps Mrs. Hernandez saw the trial as a once-(or twice-)in-a-lifetime opportunity to make friends, experience courtroom drama, and get out of her house. That impacted her thoughts, her feelings, and her actions. While she'd lost the case, she'd won time out of her house, interactions with others, and an experience she could talk about with her friends in Cuba. For her, that may have been worth it.

What They See Is What You Get

The more you can see things from other perspectives, the more likely you are to win. You can see where to put your effort and where your time would be wasted. Because when it comes to other people, what they see is what you get.

For example, my jurors often walk into the courtroom and see a terribly injured, sympathetic patient. Their thoughts, feelings, and actions might lead to a loss for me and my doctor. But if I can change what they see—to a doctor who has done her best in a world where nothing is certain and the human body is dynamic—then I can change the way they think, feel, and act, and ultimately get a win.

You can do the same. Want a raise? Help your boss see you as worth the money. Want a job? Help the interviewer see you as the best fit. Need different boundaries with a partner? Help him see how the boundaries serve him as well.

But how?

The first thing you need to know is you can't change a perspective until you understand it. And that means you can't judge their perspective. You have to work to be able to see things through another's perspective without judging what they see. That can be the hardest work of all.

Judgment is kryptonite to an advocate. If you prejudge what others see, you never get to see it yourself. And if you can't see it, you'll never change it. Let's look at the word *judgment* (as we advocates do). It comes from a Latin root that means "to form an opinion on." You know the thing about opinions, everybody's got one. Your job as an advocate is to open up and see others' perspectives without forming an opinion on them.

Here are three tools that will help you to see things from others' perspectives.

1. *Practice.*

   Start by looking at conflicts. Find one for the purposes of this exercise. It might be a conflict in your life, at work, or at home. It might be a conflict in the news. You want to see this conflict from a number of different perspectives. This is called the Villain/Victor/Victim exercise. Let's pick a conflict—like you're in a fight with your partner over who will fold and put away the laundry. Why? Because you do it every time, and you're tired of it. You just picked up his socks with a sigh, and said, "Guess I'll do this again," under your breath. And then rather than spending the night watching television together, you went to bed to read but couldn't focus because you were so frustrated by your partner's lazy, selfish ways.

   In this scenario, you see yourself as the Victim. Easy. He isn't pulling his weight, he isn't trying to help, and you have to do all the work. It's like you're a servant or something! That's the easy perspective. But let's try another.

   You are the Villain. Your poor partner doesn't mind the pile of laundry in the corner. In fact, he'd be just as happy using the pile of clothes on the floor as his new closet. No need to go searching in the back of drawers for that lost sock—they're all there, available for him to see and choose with ease. And out of nowhere you're sighing and groaning and rolling your eyes, and then you go to bed and miss the time you usually spend cuddled up watching *Parks and Recreation*. He has no idea why you're being so cold and angry, and he's suffering as a result. Can you see how this is another perspective?

Now let's try Victor. You're a laundry-folding superhero! The laundry is a challenge to overcome, and you're the one fighting and winning. Every time you fold a shirt you're not only creating an environment where you can relax and watch TV with your partner in peace, but you're also feeling good about your ability to do things you don't feel like doing. You're earning your own credibility by setting expectations (I'll fold the laundry before bed) and meeting those expectations (done!). You're winning the battle against the laundry, your self-doubt, and your laziness all in twenty minutes. Victory!

This exercise is enormously helpful in learning to see other perspectives, and the more you do it the better you get. Start small and work bigger. First it's the conflict over the laundry, then the conflict at work over credit for a recent project, and then conflict over whether you should get a raise. Once you've mastered that, you can turn to conflict over politics. Are you ready to see Trump/Obama as the Villain? It's a tough one, I know. The next tip will help.

2. *Read/watch/study all sides.*

One of the greatest gifts gained through my time on television is that it has shown me the value of this tip. I'm an equal opportunity talking head. I've done legal analysis for MSNBC, Fox News, CNN, NBC, and Newsmax. Sitting in the green rooms, talking to the guests, and watching the shows as I wait to go on has allowed me to see things from all sides of the political spectrum. Talking to the people at each station has shown me that they are good people who want the best for our country, themselves, and their families. They just have very different ideas about how to achieve the best. The more I can understand each side's ideas, the better I can help them to understand mine.

Try it. If you always read the *New York Times*, try the *Wall Street Journal* or even the *Washington Times*. If you always watch Fox News, give equal time to MSNBC. We talk a lot about the echo chamber in today's media. And it's true—when you only watch channels that you agree with, you just hear what you already know and believe. But here's the thing about this echo chamber. You can leave, for just a while. You can move around, listening for new sounds and giving them a chance. When you do, you'll start to see things from the other perspective, and then you can get to changing it.

3. *Seek out optical illusions.*
    I love optical illusions. Take a moment to google *optical illusions* and study a few. The famous ones are my favorites: I'm convinced all there is to see is two vases, until I see two faces. All I can see is the birds, until I see

a face. And I'm so focused on the old woman that the young woman is hidden to me. The feeling I get in that moment of realization that there is another way of seeing things is the feeling I want to get as often as possible when I'm advocating. And there are a lot of illusions out there. On the internet you'll see dresses of different colors depending on who you ask. And there are also audio illusions. One of my favorites is the Yanni/Laurel debate. This is where people didn't only see things differently, but they also heard them differently, too. Some people would clearly hear a male voice say, "Yanni," while others clearly heard "Laurel." When someone said they heard *Yanni* they weren't lying, wrong, or a jerk. Neither was the person who heard *Laurel*. Once we understand that, we're on our way.

The great thing about these exercises is that they help you in the worst circumstances. They illustrate the times where two perspectives are diametrically opposed. Those are the times when you have to go beyond influencing and persuading and you have to start arguing. (Argument is another tool of an advocate that we will get to.) But most of the time, that's not the case. Most of the time you don't have to destroy a juror's perspective but rather allow him to see things another way.

I always say *there's no such thing as an impartial jury*. Jurors came into my cases with their own perspectives, and that made them partial to that perspective. And your jurors are partial, too, but as long as they're also open, you've got a foot in the door. When you're advocating for what you want, it's often not so much that you have to change a perspective as you have to show the jury a new one. You want to show the jury there is more than one way of looking at things. Whether it's your Inner Jury or the Outer Jury of teammates that you want to convince, sometimes the best words that you can hear are "I've never seen it that way." That's music to your ears. Because if you've made your jury see a new way, then they can think a new way, feel a new way, act a new way, and you can get a new thing—the very thing you've been advocating for.

Precedent

This example represents one of my greatest successes as a coach. I had a client who was deathly afraid of bridges and tunnels. She hadn't driven over or in them for over fifteen years. Since she was retired, her phobia didn't impact her work, but it did impact her life. She lived in Boston and couldn't visit her family in New Hampshire because there were tunnels and bridges on the route to see them.

We talked through how if she could see tunnels and bridges from another perspective, she could choose one that worked for her. It was that of a roller coaster. She loves roller coasters. She started seeing tunnels as bridges as a fun ride, the way she saw a roller coaster.

This change in perspective completely changed her life. She visits her family in New Hampshire. And she has a new part-time job as an Uber driver!

Summary of the Case: Perspective

1. *What you see is what you get.* The STEER process shows us this with Sight/Thought/Emotion/Action/Reaction, Result, and Response. Choose what you see, and you can change what you get.

2. *Everyone has his truth.* When you realize that truth is simply a belief with evidence to support it, you recognize that you can change a person's truth using the tools of an advocate. And that person could be you.

3. *Practice seeing other people's perspectives.* Use the Rose/Bud/Thorn exercise or the Villain/Victor/Victim exercise to start to get good at seeing all the perspectives available to you.

Chapter 4
Questions

Tell me.

I became an advocate in fourth grade.

At the time I didn't know I was advocating.

An advocate is "someone who publicly supports something." Back then, I used a question to publicly support a classmate. Many years later, I'd discover that questions were one of the main tools of an advocate.

I went to Catholic school, and I was in a small class where the students had all known each other since first grade. But that year, there was a new girl in school. Anna was beautiful, and she looked and acted much older than the rest of us. She carried a purple purse that went over her shoulder, and she'd fling it on with a flip of her hair. The girls in my class were all immediately entranced with this girl who knew, said, and did things we didn't. Anna became the queen of the class, and everyone wanted her favor.

But Anna could be mean.

There was a boy on our bus who was in second grade and he was awkward. He talked too loudly, said the wrong things, and was often the butt of the jokes. He was one of the last people to get on the bus, which meant that there weren't many seats by the time he climbed those steep stairs and brushed past the driver. Every day he'd look around nervously, hoping to make it to an empty seat before anyone attacked him. Whether he made it each day was a crapshoot.

On one particular day, he didn't make it past Anna's row of wrath.

Anna must have been upset about something (hurt people hurt people) and she went too far. The boy hadn't even taken his seat before she made fun of his looks, his lisp, and his love of science fiction. She went deep. I sat and listened, but I didn't speak up. I was afraid. I didn't want Anna to turn her attention to me and attack me as well.

At first it was easy just to sit there and keep quiet, let someone else bear the brunt of her fury. But then something changed that made me an advocate that day. It wasn't her cruelty that prompted me to act. It was eye contact. Just as another one of Anna's attacks hit this young boy, I made eye contact with him. I saw the pain in his eyes, and once I saw that pain, I couldn't unsee it. I had to speak.

"What are you doing?" I asked her.

That's all I could think to say. What was she doing? She was torturing this young boy. She was hurting him. Some part of me wanted to know if she knew that.

I remember quaking while I waited for her to respond. I was still sitting in the rough green school bus seat, peering at Anna over the tall back. In my fourth-grade mind everyone was looking at me in shock and disgust. I was terrified that Anna would turn her sharp tongue on me next.

"What do you mean *what am I doing*?" she asked.

"What are you doing? I'm just wondering." It was all I could think to say.

Anna and I made eye contact, and something in that moment made her stop.

"Nothing." And with that, she moved on to talking about what happened on *Who's the Boss?* the night before.

Anna was being a bully, but that one question stopped her, at least for the moment. That's because questions have enormous power.

More often than not when I told people I was a trial attorney someone inevitably said, "Oh, I should have been a trial attorney. I'm great at arguing." I immediately know that person would likely make a terrible trial attorney. We don't argue to win. In jury trials, the opening statement is just that—a statement. It's actually meant to be an outline of the case, and an attorney can get reprimanded by the judge if she argues during her opening. The closing argument is just that—an argument. That's when we get to argue. But closing arguments are a small fraction of the trial. The rest of the trial, day in and day out, the way we win is by…asking questions.

"Ms. Hansen," a judge would say, "your witness."

That means it's my witness to question. It's my witness to use to prove something or support something. It's my witness to build and buttress, or it's my witness to challenge and attack. I get to do what I want with this witness, as long as I do it with questions. It turns out you can do almost anything with questions. You can make a jury love or hate a witness. You can build credibility or take it away. You can create emotion, establish scientific principles, and build connections.

Questions work just as well outside the courtroom. You, too, can use questions to create connections, to build credibility, and to challenge. You can even stop a bully.

You can use questioning tools to advocate to allies and enemies, depending on what you want to accomplish. But remember—the most important jury you have to influence and persuade is your Inner Jury. You can use questions to persuade that jury as well.

Question the Inner Voices, Too

When the voices inside your head start their racket, you have to question them. You can't just assume what they say is true.

"He thinks you're silly."

"You'll never do it."

"You're too old, too young, too shy, too aggressive…"

The Inner Jury is listening to all the voices in your head. Some of them can be bullies as well. But remember, what you see is what you get. Your job as an advocate is to change what the jury sees. Questions are what helps you do that. It means you have to be aware of what you see and what that Inner Jury is telling you. Because, as I've said, you have to understand the perspective to change it.

Awareness is key. And once you're aware, you start asking.

"When did he say he thought I'm silly?"

"What evidence supports the conclusion that I'll never do it?"

"Did you hear him say that was a great presentation?"

"Do you remember when he asked you to be on his team?"

All these questions could help you change perspective.

"Why would you think that?"

In the chapter on words we talked about "why" and how that word puts people on the defense. But in some situations, like when your Inner Jury is trying to decide whether to choose judgmental voices, it is a good word. Put that jury of voices in your head on the defense. Make them defend their thoughts and provide evidence. Chances are they can't, and now you have a new perspective.

When the voices inside your head get really aggressive, you can use the same question I used with the school bus bully. "What are you doing?" Sometimes that's enough to see that you're really just beating yourself up, entertaining your ego, or creating an excuse not to act. And those answers, too, will help you to see things differently.

Questioning Others

Once you've overcome the voices in your head, questioning anyone else is a cakewalk. You can use questions to prove your point, challenge an adversary, create connection, and reach an accord. Questions are the key in negotiations and during argument. They are your Swiss army knife. But to use them you have to remember that they're in your pocket.

During my keynote speeches, often people forget about questions. Before we were faced with a pandemic and touching each other became verboten, I used to ask people to clasp hands with the person next to them, leaving their thumb free and facing upward. Then I ask them to get their partner's thumb down. I give them some time and then try to get their attention back. (People love to play thumb war! But I don't call it war so that my audience doesn't assume that violence is the only way to win.) Then I ask those who were successful in getting their partner's hand down to tell me how they did it.

"I used brute force."

"I distracted her with conversation and then got her."

"I'm really fast and just didn't give him a chance to think."

Then I ask, "Did anyone just ask their partner to put their thumb down?" And in all the thousands of people I've presented to, not one person has raised their hand.

Questions are one of our strongest tools, yet most people forget to use them.

But we have to remember. *Questions can help us prevent war.* They do so when we use them to explore whether we're missing anything. While training as a mediator I learned the perfect example of this theory. It's the story of the Case of the Orange. In this case, the two sides were fighting over a perfect orange. It was plump and appeared to be juicy, with the perfect color rind, completely round, and without a single bump or divot. Both sides wanted this orange so badly that they brought suit over it and ended up at a mediator's office. The mediator spent all day going back and forth between the two parties, who were in separate rooms with their respective attorneys, but neither side was willing to compromise. They both wanted all or nothing. The mediator tried threats, begging, and evidence. He was exhausted. Finally, at the end of the day he came into the room where the first party had camped out for the day. He was exhausted and ready to quit. Then he asked a question.

"Why do you want this orange so much?"

"I'm a bartender, and I make award-winning cocktails. I want that beautiful rind as a garnish for my cocktails to use in my new book of my concoctions."

The mediator suddenly woke up. He scurried into the other room, where the attorneys and their client were packing up their bags.

"Wait, why do you want this orange so badly?"

"I own a health food store and I'm creating Instagram ads. I know the juice of this orange would help me create a picture that would get a million likes."

And with that, resolution. The bartender got his rind, the juicer got her juice, and the mediator got his lesson. *Questions are magic.*

In that mediation, questions overcame the curse of knowledge. The bartender knew why he wanted the orange, and it didn't occur to him to say it was for the rind. He had the curse of knowledge. The juicer didn't think to say she wanted just the juice—she knew what she wanted and didn't realize that others didn't. She had the curse as well. Remember the patient who didn't know what an MRI was? In that case the doctor had the curse. He knew what an MRI was, and he knew it so well that he forgot what it was like not to know it. How do you break the curse? With questions.

If the patient in that case had asked, "What is an MRI?" there likely would have been no lawsuit, and perhaps no deadly conclusion to that story. If the doctor had asked, "Do you understand?" or "Do you have any questions?"—same end result.

By now you likely agree that questions have power, and you may be asking some. The most common is "What should I ask?"

Here are three very powerful questions, and the best time to use them.

Three Key Questions to Use to Advocate

1. *What am I missing?*
    This might be my favorite question of all time. It overcomes the curse of knowledge. If either the doctor or the patient had asked that question, curse broken. It also allows us to remind ourselves and others that there's always another way of looking at things. There's always another perspective. When you ask, "What am I missing?" of yourself, you suddenly start looking around for new evidence, new information, and new perspectives. And if you keep asking it, you get creative. When I'm preparing for a trial I ask this question of my team over and over again. They know that I expect an answer other than "nothing" or "I don't know." I expect creativity, attention to detail, and preparation. Often I find that what I'm missing is what allows us to win the case.

    When you ask this of someone else, you give them some power. First, it shows some humility. It's like the *owning it* piece of credibility. By asking, "What am I missing?" you're admitting that you know you could be missing something. You're acknowledging that you aren't perfect. In doing so, you make the other side more likely to share things they may not have. Suddenly, you're not missing a thing.

I get frustrated when people don't use this question well. In trial, there is only one guaranteed opportunity to question the jury. *Voir dire* is the name of the process by which we choose our jury for our trials. During voir dire I could ask prospective jurors questions about their experiences, their background, and their biases. But during the entire trial, I couldn't ask the jury a single question, and that put me at a huge disadvantage. I wanted to ask my jury what they saw, what they heard, what they wanted to know and why. There's no chance of it in court. But you can do it in life. You can ask your jury of clients, customers, investors, or teammates, "What am I missing?" And you can use the answer to help you win.

Try this one anytime you're confused. Have it in your back pocket to use whenever you're about to make a final conclusion or take a major step. It helps to step back, change perspectives, and build a connection with the person you're asking.

2. *What are you doing?*

This is a great question to use to challenge someone. You can ask it of yourself and the negative voices inside your head anytime they've gone off on an unproductive tangent, and you can use it when they're bullying you into submission. This question creates a pause and slows things down. It allows someone (maybe you) to recognize that she's not acting with elegance or intent, and to choose differently.

As demonstrated with the school bus story, it works with bullies. It's also a useful question to memorize and practice with so that it comes out when you're feeling threatened. In my book *The Elegant Warrior*, Chapter 5 is called "Decide Whether to Get Dirty." In that chapter I tell the story of one of my many #MeToo moments in the courtroom. In that story my response to such a moment was to call out the men involved by saying, "I don't think that's funny." Hundreds of women have reached out to me about that chapter, wondering how I maintained my elegance enough to know what to say. My honest answer is I don't know how I did it that time. I think it was intuition and a little divine intervention. But I now know how to handle stressful, difficult conversations. I practice, and I recommend you do the same.

Have this question ready the next time someone disrespects you, bullies you, or harasses you. First of all, when someone is doing something wrong, this question often makes them recognize it. Simply asking the question is often enough to stop the behavior. Second, it's not as threatening or challenging to the perpetrator as a direct response. In those situations where you are the person who isn't in power, either physically or via status, challenge doesn't always feel safe. Questions feel safer. The third reason to use this question is that it often allows others to advocate for you as well. I think one of the reasons Anna stopped bullying that boy on the bus was that she saw the other students thinking, "What is she doing?" With numbers, the power can shift.

Practice this one. Have your kids practice it, too. This question can help turn a lot of scary situations into realizations.

3. *Tell me...*

When Judge Aquilina spoke to the women who'd been abused by Nassar, she would say, "Tell me what you want me to know." While you might not see that as a question, it's close enough and is similar in spirit. It's a request for information, and as we saw in that case, it has the power to change lives. Much of that power lies in the fact that she gave the power back to the women—it was what they wanted her to know. Broken down, the first two words hold the power: Tell me.

What if your child stayed out past curfew? The next morning when you're having a conversation about it, you may ask why. The child will likely feel defensive. If you say, "Tell me what you were thinking," it's different. "Tell me" opens things up a little. It sounds more curious. It sounds less like an attack and more like the request that it is. "Tell me" sounds like you believe the person has her reasons and you want to hear them. It gives the person who is answering the space to...tell you.

In response to "tell me" you'll get much more evidence, much more perspective. You'll see much more in response. I've never done a formal experiment on this, but in over twenty years in the courtroom I've done an informal one on these two words. When I asked a witness, "What happened?" I got a certain answer. But when I asked a witness to "tell the jury what happened," I got more—more detail, more reasons, more evidence, and more perspective. "Tell me" opens the door to a greater explanation.

On cross-examination that's a lot. There's a reason that poker players refer to the unconscious behavior that gives a clue to their hand as a *tell*. The more time a person takes to answer a question, the more that person is giving you body language, facial expression, and tone of voice to read. The longer anyone talks, the more information you get. "Tell me" gets people talking.

These three questions can help you advocate and help you win. A question is magic because it's a Trojan Horse. There are times I've cross-examined people so well that they had no idea they'd been made to look a fool until the jury started laughing. In those times, my clients often wanted to high-five me afterward. But I remind my clients in every trial—the enemy isn't that expert, the patient who sued them, or even opposing counsel. The enemy for every advocate is misunderstanding. The best way to slay that enemy is with questions.

Let Your Outer Jury Figure It Out

Questions work well because your Outer Jury would prefer to believe that they've figured things out rather than believing that you told them something. When your Outer Jury believes something, and owns that belief, they're the best advocates you could imagine. You have questions, let your Outer Jury have the answers. That's how you turn anyone, including your adversaries, into your advocates.

I didn't understand this when I was a young attorney. When you're an attorney in training, you serve as second chair on your cases. That means usually you don't ask any questions or make any arguments, but you organize exhibits, prepare examinations, and, most importantly, you watch. I had the distinct privilege of watching John O'Brien try his cases for years before I ever tried my first case. I'd prepare direct or cross-examinations for him, and he'd tweak them (and often rewrite them completely) and then use them to question the witness. But he'd almost always cut the question I'd written where I'd wanted to tell the jury what was going on.

"So, Doctor, you're telling me there's no way that this patient is actually suffering from the nerve injury she claims?"

In John's hands, that question was always removed. He'd draw a big red line right through it. I never understood why. I used my tool of Questions and asked him. He told me that juries like to figure things out on their own. They like their own creations. And you should never tell them something that they could figure (and likely had figured) out themselves.

I respected his intellect and his experience, but some part of me didn't agree. I was afraid that some of the jurors hadn't figured it out, and if we didn't tell them they never would. But I underestimated John and I underestimated the jury and the power of a strong advocate. One day, though, I got it. We'd tried a complicated surgical case to verdict. In my opinion the patient had clearly been lying to the jury and to some of her doctors. I wanted John to make that clearer than I thought he had. He told me the jury got it. At the end of the case, we won and the jury wanted to talk to the lawyers. The foreman of the jury dominated the conversation.

"I knew she was lying, man. You know, in the records in her own handwriting she circled a big smiling face when the nurse asked her to rate her pain. A smiling face! But now she's telling us she was in ten out of ten pain that day? Come on, man. I'm too smart for that. And when some of these guys [pointing at the other jurors] didn't remember, I reminded them of that. Because I hate liars, and she was clearly lying."

John was right. We didn't have to call her a liar. We just had to ask the right questions to make at least one juror call her a liar. And when he did, he'd advocate for what he'd found. Questions are the secret to doing that. You're not telling anyone anything. You're just exploring, unearthing treasure, and letting people believe they're the ones who've found it.

And research backs John up. In a study titled *IKEA Effect*, researchers at Harvard Business School found that people overvalue the things on which they have labored. My favorite part of this study was about origami.[9] The researchers asked some participants to make origami animals and then to place a value on those animals. Others had to place a value on animals they didn't make. Those who created the origami put a much higher value on the animals than those who did not. Just as John had told me, people like their own creations. They put a greater value on them.

When it's our own conviction or creation, we are more willing to advocate for it.

<hr>

[9]   Michael I. Norton, Daniel Mochon, and Dan Ariely, "The IKEA Effect: When Labor Leads to Love," *Journal of Consumer Psychology* 22, no. 3 (July 2012): 453–460.

Your Witness

My final (and likely most important) tip about questions should go without saying, but it doesn't.

Don't be afraid to ask them, even if they are simple.

When the judge said, "Your witness," it was my turn. It didn't matter if I wasn't ready or if I didn't think I had all my ducks in a little row. I had no choice but to stand up and start asking questions. And sometimes I'd purposefully ask the most basic question. Remember, everyone knows something that someone else doesn't. I'd ask questions for each juror. I'd ask questions for myself. At depositions I'd ask the most basic questions to be sure I had the information right, so that at trial I'd be asking the questions that best served me and my clients. For a lawyer, asking questions is a sign of strength, intelligence, and capability.

You need to see it that way, too.

Studies show that people who ask for advice are seen as *more* competent than those who don't.[10] And people think you're especially smart when you choose them to ask for advice. The thinking is that asking for help demonstrates smarts. Asking questions makes you look curious, industrious, and smart.

Once my trials start, I don't get to turn to the jury and say, "Tell me what you want to know." Or "How am I doing?" I don't

---

[10]   Karen Huang, Michael Yeomans, Alison Wood Brooks, Julia Minson, and Francesca Gino, "It Doesn't Hurt to Ask: Question-Asking Increases Liking," *Journal of Personality and Social Psychology* 113, no. 3 (September 2017): 430–452.

get to ask, "Does this make sense?" or "What am I missing?" And I don't get to ask them for advice. "What would you ask this witness?" But I wish I did. If I could ask the jury questions, I'd know where to focus. I'd know what they need and want to hear. I'd know how to win. You have that opportunity when you are advocating, so I urge you to use it.

Ask your Outer Jury questions.

If it's your customers, ask them what works and what doesn't. Use polls, research, and especially use conversations. Twenty minutes of conversation with your clients or customers can be the most valuable part of your day if you're asking the right questions and truly receiving the answers. (Reception is so important that it's a tool on its own.)

And for women reading this: you need to recognize that women are less likely to ask than men are.

Ask. Ask more. Ask *for* more.

In a study of 250 events at thirty-five institutions across ten countries, Alecia Carter and her coauthors wrote that women are two and a half times less likely to ask a question in an academic department seminar than men.[11] These were women across different institutions and different countries. Their reasons included not feeling smart enough or feeling intimidated.

But I think there's something else going on. At least there was for me.

Once I decided to start advocating for myself, I had to overcome a real aversion to asking for what I wanted. And for me the

---

[11]   Alecia J. Carter, Alyssa Croft, Dieter Lukas, Gillian M. Sandstrom, "Women's Visibility in Academic Seminars: Women Ask Fewer Questions Than Men," *PLOS ONE* 14(2), 2019.

fear was not that I wasn't smart enough. It was that I was being needy. I wanted to be seen as strong, independent, and sure. Needy was for damsels in distress, and I certainly didn't want to be seen as in distress. I thought I should be able to do it all myself and that others were doing it all themselves. I thought it wasn't elegant to ask. My biggest problem was that I thought other people should know what I wanted and needed and want to give it to me.

Part of me also felt that I shouldn't have to ask. I thought my partner, my boss, my client, or my customer should be able to intuit what I wanted and needed and then give it to me. Since I thought I'd earned it, I deserved what I wanted. I believed they should see that and give it to me.

That thinking is nothing short of ridiculous. I realized that during one of my trials. At the end of every case, I stand before the jury and ask them to give me a win. I ask them to enter a verdict on behalf of my doctor or hospital. And my ask is as clear as day. I tell them.

"I ask you to enter a verdict on behalf of Dr. Smith."

I show them. I actually take the verdict sheet they will be using and show them exactly where I want them to mark. I couldn't be clearer. And I realized that when I'm advocating for myself and my needs, I need to be just as clear. Clarity wins. Because people don't know what you want if you don't tell them.

First of all, very few people are that emotionally aware and intelligent. Most people are so focused on their own feelings, fears, and wants that they aren't tuned in to other people's feelings. But more than that, you know what you want better than anyone. You know the nuances of what you want—I want more money, but time with my family is even more important. I want you to rub my back, but softly and with just your fingertips. The only way you're going to get what you want is to ask for it, with specificity. Show people what you want, with clarity and specificity. Get out a piece of paper. Write it down. The more ways you tell your Outer Jury how to give you what you want, the more likely you are to receive it.

Create a Question Journal

The only way you'll get good at asking for what you want is by practicing. One of the best ways to become better at asking questions is a question journal. Get a journal. At the beginning of each day, write down three questions you intend to ask by the end of the day. They have to be specific. And then…ask them. At the end of the day, record your answers. This will make asking questions a habit for you, but it will also make you ask better questions. Over time you'll see what kinds of questions are working best for you. You'll start to come up with questions you love and others that don't work for you. And you'll see that the answers you're getting are getting you what you want.

You can also do this before any meeting/date/interaction. Write down three questions you want answered by the end of the meeting or the date. Then put the list in your pocket and, over the course of your time together, ask them. You'll find this practice makes you less nervous, as you have questions prepared to fall back on. It often makes me even more excited for the meeting or the date because I know I'm going to learn something. And for those of you who are single, studies show that when it comes to speed dating, the ones who ask the most questions get the most second dates.

So please, will you start asking questions? Could you start today and ask more questions than you feel comfortable asking? And would you let me know how it goes?

Precedent

In my coaching practice, I have a client who is a well-known surgeon. He heard me give a keynote and hired me shortly thereafter to coach him. During that keynote, I told the group about a study that showed that if everyone in the operating room knows everyone else's names, there are fewer complications during the surgery.[12] I recommended that the group ask more questions, starting with a simple one, "What's your name?"

This client took that advice to heart, and he started asking everyone's name before every operation he performed. That led to a drop in complications, not to mention better relationships among the operating room staff. Oddly enough, those shifts led to this surgeon wanting to ask even more questions. Our work together is primarily focused on giving him the skills he needs to ask the best questions, at work and at home. Not only does he feel this has improved his patients' care, but he also feels it has benefited his marriage, his family, and his own self-awareness. Questions really are magic.

---

[12] "Atul Gawande's 'Checklist' for Surgery Success," NPR Author Interviews, January 5, 2010.

Summary of the Case: Questions

1. *You get to ask the questions.* Let your jury have the answers. Everyone likes to have the answers. We like to feel smart, special, and significant, and having answers lets us feel all three. You be the one to ask the questions and let your jury answer.

2. *How can I see this differently?* This is the best question to use with your Inner Jury. It opens things up and reminds you of another tool (Perspective). Ask yourself this question anytime you're feeling defeated, and not only will you stop feeling that way, you'll also start winning.

3. *Tell me.* Start more conversations with these two words and your life will magically change.

Chapter 5
Credibility

You can't advocate until you believe.

"We didn't like your client. But we believed you."

I realized the power of credibility early in my career during an obstetric case involving the birth of triplets. During the very difficult delivery, one of the triplets died. One had been born with severe damages, and one was born healthy. That's a compelling story to tell if you're the attorney for the triplets and their parents. You can compare the surviving children and go through the milestones that only one child will reach. Most of the jury will have children, and so you can speak to their experience as parents and what it would be like to watch one child progress while the other didn't, knowing that a third never even had the chance. The attorney for the family could talk about steps never taken, a solo birthday cake where there were meant to be three, and high school graduations where the futures couldn't be any more different. It was a gripping tale.

The attorneys for the defendants had a very different tale to tell. I represented the obstetrician, but the family also sued a maternal fetal medicine doctor who had treated the mother throughout her pregnancy, the resident physicians (physicians in training), and the nurses who had attended to the mother throughout her labor. Other attorneys represented each of the other defendants. We didn't have as compelling a story. Instead, we had complicated medical terms, an unusual diagnosis, and complex fetal monitoring strips to explain.

My client, the obstetrician, was gruff. She didn't have a lot of patience for me or the case. When I asked her to explain the fetal monitoring strips to me, she told me a child could understand fetal monitoring strips. Well, not me—not when I was a child, and not that day. I knew the jury wouldn't understand either and that if she maintained that attitude we were heading for a loss.

I understand when my clients are frustrated and angry. One of my superpowers is that I can see things from almost anyone's perspective, and I saw this case through hers. She'd depended on the maternal fetal medicine doctor and the hospital staff to inform her of certain findings. They hadn't. My doctor was angry at them and herself for not asking more questions. She was protective of them as well. This was her team, after all. And she felt unbelievably guilty about the outcome. She knew, and I knew, that she'd done everything within the standard of care to deliver three healthy babies. She'd done everything right. But an obstetrician goes to work to give life, not to take it, and she had to live with this outcome forever. All this made her appear angry, defensive, and dismissive. Not a great formula to win a case. However, we did have the medicine on our side. We had a strong and likable expert. And I did everything I could to build our credibility with the jury.

The verdict was complicated. The jury found against the maternal fetal medicine doctor and awarded the family an astronomical sum. But they found in favor of my client, the residents, and the nurses. The trial had been exhausting, three and a half weeks of sleepless nights and stressful days. We'd won a case I hadn't dared to believe we could win. The jury wanted to talk to the lawyers.

This happens. Many judges give jurors the option of talking to the attorneys when the case is over. And after long cases like this one, the jurors often take the judges up on that offer. We've worked together, laughed together, and cried together for more than three weeks. They want to talk.

The family's attorney entered the room first, fresh off his win and the eight figures he'd be taking home as a result. His defense attorneys followed, as did I, and counsel for the residents and nurses, and then the attorney for the maternal fetal medicine doctor. (I did not envy that attorney.) The jurors asked their questions about the case, the experts, the witnesses, and the attorneys. I was the only female attorney in the room and, as was often the case back then, the jurors had questions about why I always wore my hair up and why I only wore pantsuits. That was nothing new, and it didn't bother me. But then I heard a comment I'd never heard before, and one that would influence how I advocated forever thereafter.

"You know, we didn't like your doctor. Hated her. But we believed you."

Credibility won. They believed me.

Credibility wins in the courtroom. And credibility wins outside the courtroom as well. If you want to win—sales, attention, loyalty, or engagement, respect, influence, or healthy boundaries—you've got to be credible.

Bottom line: you can't win if your Outer Jury doesn't believe, and they won't believe if you aren't credible. If the people you want to influence and persuade don't find you credible, you lose. Credibility is the foundation, and it's where you can build your authenticity, your vulnerability, your likability, and ultimately your trust. But credibility has to come first.

Facts tell, stories sell, but advocates win.

Any time you have two competing stories, the story that people believe is the story that will win. And there are always competing stories. The story of why you should get the promotion competes against the story of why someone else should get it. The story of why your client should hire you versus the story of why they should hire a competitor. The story of why your child should eat his vegetables versus the story of why she prefers candy. All these are competing stories. Your job as an advocate is to craft the story that your jury believes. You have got to be credible.

Vulnerability, Authenticity, and Trust

As I coach people on the topic of credibility, they sometimes try to convince me that some other trend is more important than credibility. For a while, the big buzzword out there was *authenticity*. "But I have to be authentic!" Then it was *vulnerability*. "I need to be vulnerable here." And *trust*, of course, is a term often bandied about for leaders and those in sales. "How can I make them trust me?" But while vulnerability, authenticity, and trust are all valuable in their own ways and at their own time, credibility always comes first.

Let's examine vulnerability. *Vulnerability* is defined as "the state of being exposed to harm," and the root of the word is "wounded." That's not something I urge my clients to embrace, not in the courtroom or in the boardroom. In the courtroom my clients are vulnerable, no doubt. When they get up onto the witness stand to advocate for themselves and what they did, they're exposing themselves to an adverse verdict and so they're exceedingly vulnerable. But we don't focus on vulnerability, and we sure don't aim for it. In the boardroom my client may be about to be fired, demoted, or criticized. That feels vulnerable, too. Any time your money, your ego, or your relationships are at stake you are potentially exposing yourself to harm. No one wants their ideas, passion, income, or potential to be "wounded." It's not what we're going for, especially in professional situations. I think vulnerability is best suited for personal relationships. We must be open to being wounded when we're sharing our hearts, our fears, and our greatest dreams. And that happens most often in personal relationships. I'm also not saying that vulnerability never has a place when you're advocating. I'm saying credibility comes first.

Authenticity is a little different. It has many definitions, but one is really on trend right now. That definition of *authenticity* is "true to one's personality, spirit, or character," and the origin is "authentikos," or "genuine." Sounds good, right? But I don't encourage people to lead with authenticity either. Authenticity doesn't win. If someone took the stand in trial and said to the jury, "I'm scared you'll find against me," or "I'm mad that patient sued me," that would be authentic. But it wouldn't help our case. Jurors don't care what witnesses genuinely feel if it's irrelevant to the case at hand. The jury does want to know if they can believe. And your Outer Jury wants to know the same.

You won't win with authenticity either. If you're authentically feeling angry, cranky, or bored, you don't want to start declaring it to your investors or your clients. In fact, you are more likely to be successful in your career if you're able to manage others' impressions of you.[13] When you manage impressions, you're not being authentic. You might be authentically showing who you want to be or who you aspire to be, but you're not always being authentic to who you are in the moment. Aspirational authenticity—being true to one's potential—certainly could help you advocate. That's elegance, and it's an advocate's tool that we've already discussed. But authenticity as it is generally used isn't the key to winning. Before you can be authentic, you have to make them believe. Credibility comes first.

Finally, you may have heard that trust will bring you success. I am frequently reminded by people I coach that they want to have trust with their clients, customers, and team members, and of course they do. *Trust* is defined as a "firm belief in the reliability, truth, ability, or strength of something." And the root of the word is "strong." I'd aspire to that, and I bet you would, too. But trust takes time. You have to earn trust, with repeated

---

13   Dimitri van der Linden et al., "Overlap between the General Factor of Personality and Emotional Intelligence: A Meta-Analysis," *Psychological Bulletin* 143, no. 1 (2017): 36–52, https://psycnet.apa.org/buy/2016-55071-001.

right action. In business and in life you don't always have the time for trust.

I definitely didn't have that kind of time in my trials. Some of my trials took two weeks; some took two days. That wasn't enough time for my jury to trust me. It's wasn't enough time to earn their trust. And you don't have time either. You need a new job—*now*. You need investors—*now*. You need customers you just met to buy—*now*. And you need clients you just encountered to engage—*now*. You don't have time to build trust. That can come later. But you have time for credibility. Credibility always comes first. Trust follows, and guess what follows trust? Confidence. The root of the word *confidence* is "confidere," which means to "have full trust." Confidence has to be based on trust, and trust has to be based on credibility. Again: credibility always comes first.

You have to make them believe. Belief is enormously powerful. It wins cases and it wins hearts. One study illustrates the power of belief in an unbelievable way. In this study, Japanese researchers studied thirteen boys who were hypersensitive to the leaves of the Japanese wax trees. (These trees produce effects similar to poison ivy.) The researchers touched the students on one arm with leaves from a harmless tree but told them that these were poisonous leaves; they then touched the students on the other arm with poisonous leaves but told them that the leaves were harmless. All thirteen arms touched with the harmless leaves showed a skin reaction, but only two touched with the poisonous leaves did so. In this study the harmless leaves not only induced a dramatic skin reaction, but also that reaction was greater than the one produced by the poisonous leaves. According to this study, the mere thought that one is being touched with a poisonous leaf can bring on a skin eruption.[14]

Read that again. The boys broke out in a rash because they believed a harmless leaf was poison ivy. That's the power of belief. It creates biological reactions. Let's use that power in a positive way to advocate.

The definition of *credibility* is "the quality of being believed." The origin of the word is "credere" ("believe"). Everyone is just looking for something to believe in. You have to make it you. When people believe in something, they're far more likely to share it. When they believe in something, they're more likely to buy. And when they believe in something, they become advocates. You can't advocate until you believe. Your job is to make your jury believe in you.

Believe in You

If you can't advocate until you believe, then you've got to believe in yourself, your worth, your wants, your needs, and your business before you can advocate for them. Your Inner Jury has to choose. You've got to believe so strongly that you're ready to go out and make others believe as well. This is something that many of us struggle with.

Your Inner Jury has to choose to believe in you. She has to believe that you can take the gifts the Universe gives you and use them to get what you want. Believe in yourself first and act on

---

14   Walter A. Brown, "Expectation, the Placebo Effect and the Response to Treatment," *Rhode Island Medical Journal* (May 2015).

that belief. It's the only way to get what you want. It's also the best way to build your own credibility.

When you're building credibility, whether with your Inner or Outer Jury, this three-step process is the same.

1. *Make promises and keep them.*

   This is the verbal part of credibility. When you make a promise, you've got to keep it. So first consider your promises. Whenever I make a promise I first consider, "Could I do this? Am I capable of keeping this promise?" If the answer is yes, the next question is, "Will I do this?" We are capable of almost anything, but that doesn't mean we'll do it. You have to be honest with yourself when you answer this question. Before you make a promise, you have to believe that you can and will keep it.

   And then, you do. That often means choosing discomfort. I lost a hundred pounds in the early '90s, and I did it by promising myself I'd do something physical five days a week. I promised myself I'd eat three proteins, one fruit, two starches, and unlimited vegetables a day. I promised myself I'd stay away from sugar. And I kept those promises. It wasn't always easy. Some days it was hard. But my mantra about hard things is: "You could do it anyway." Everything is a choice, and it was harder to break a promise to myself than to follow that program.

   And the benefits were amazing. It wasn't just that every time I kept a promise, I got closer to my goal weight. It was that every time I kept a promise, I found myself feeling more credible. I started to believe in myself and the promises I made to myself. I earned my credibility, which led to earning my trust and then my self-confidence. That has made me a better advocate. You can't advocate until you believe.

2. *Set expectations and meet them.*

You set expectations for yourself every day. You expect to get up at six, move your body, and get to work by nine. And you consistently do so. That consistency leads to more expectation—since you do something the majority of the time, you expect that you will do that thing. When it comes to earning credibility with your Inner Jury, you want to be aware of the expectations your actions are setting and be sure that they serve you.

With your Outer Jury, the process is the same. If your partner is always late for dates, you expect him to be late for dates. He hasn't promised to be late for dates, and in fact he's likely promised *not* to be. But he's set a certain expectation, for better or worse. Another example is that friend who can't keep a secret. Even if she promises to keep a secret, once she's set the expectation that she won't, it will be hard for her to overcome.

You can set positive expectations as well. I do this all the time in the courtroom. I believe the courtroom and the trials we hold in that room are sacrosanct. I believe that everyone who steps into that room has dignity and deserves respect. I respect the parties and the process. And I act that way. I set an expectation for myself that I won't yell or have a tantrum in the courtroom. I also don't joke around a lot or even laugh a lot in the courtroom. For me, every trial is serious. And by acting with dignity, respect, and elegance every time I step into the courtroom, I manage others' expectations as well.

Judges expect me to act a certain way, as do opposing counsel. The jury starts to expect the same. They see me every day, dignified and elegant even when opposing counsel yells, throws things, or makes snide comments. The longer the trial goes, the more the jury's expectation grows. And when I meet that expectation every day, I am building credibility with myself and with them. I have to make sure I can and will meet the expectation.

Another expectation I set for myself is that I'll be the first lawyer to the courtroom. I know that I can be—no matter what time the others get there, I just have to get there earlier. But will I? For me, this is easy. I'm an early riser, and I always overestimate how long it will take me to get places. But for some of my fellow lawyers this expectation is too hard. They don't get up early, and they won't be first to arrive. They shouldn't set the expectation, mainly because the first day they miss it they'll have lost a little belief in themselves. And that loss of credibility matters.

3. *Own it.*

This step is all about being honest with yourself and with others. There will be times when you won't meet your own expectations or keep your promises to yourself. Don't just brush over those instances. Don't ignore them and pretend they didn't happen. You have to recognize when you've missed the mark so that you'll be less likely to miss in the future, but also so that you can trust yourself that you'll tell yourself the truth.

This is the secret sauce of building credibility with others as well. Because there will be times when you can't keep your promises or meet your expectations, and that is when you have to own it. This is what I think people mean when they talk about vulnerability and authenticity. Owning it means you are open to being wounded and being genuine about your shortcomings. Owning it means you admit when you didn't keep a promise or meet an expectation. Just the act of owning it can give you huge credibility with yourself and with your jury.

One of the doctors I used as an expert is fabulous at this. He's so good at it that he will purposefully not keep a promise or not meet an expectation just so that he can own it and build credibility with the jury. In one case he was the expert for the defense. As such, it was his job to defend the actions of the defendant doctor. Most of the time experts for a doctor will agree with everything the defendant doctor says. They, and the defense lawyers, often believe that the fewer the contradictions, the greater the credibility. I disagreed, and so did this expert.

During our prep session we went through the defendant doctor's deposition. The doctor had been questioned for hours about his treatment and why he chose the treatment plan he did. The expert agreed with everything the defendant doctor said, until we came to page 143 of the deposition. The expert paused and said, "This isn't right. I don't agree with what he said here." And I said, "Well, then say that."

Fortunately, it wasn't a major point. And even more important, it had no impact on whether the doctor had caused the patient's injury. But it was a contradiction. And while I'd never promised that our expert and our defendant doctor would agree on everything, it was what the jury expected. It was what opposing counsel expected. By not meeting that expectation and owning it rather than trying to dance around it or avoid the question, we built huge amounts of credibility with the jury. Sometimes my clients want to fight every point on cross-examination. And I understand. But I try to make them understand that by honestly ceding a point or two and owning some things that may hurt a little, they're building huge amounts of credibility with the jury.

There are so many ways you can own it. One of my favorite ways is saying, "I don't know." As a partner in my law firm, I depended on my associates and paralegals to provide me with answers. And often when there was an unusual legal question they'd say, "I'll have the answer to you by Monday." When Monday came, they might not have been able to keep that promise. Maybe the answer wasn't clear. Maybe they were sick all weekend and not up to the task of analyzing all the case law. Maybe they just didn't know. The best thing that I could hear on Monday morning is, "I don't know the answer." That's owning it. And it's hard. The more you're willing to admit you don't know or you were wrong or you don't understand, the faster you'll build credibility.

But it doesn't stop there. If you want to gain huge amounts of credibility you have to go further and fix it.

The most credible associates are those who say, "I don't know...but I did this research, wrote this memo, asked this other partner, and have these ideas." Now their credibility has gone through the roof.

And you can do the same. Say, "I don't know...but I'll find out." "I was wrong...and here is what I plan to do to make it better." "I made a mistake...and this is how I will fix it." "I don't understand...but I'm going to sit down and listen to you until I do." Just typing these words gets me excited for you. If you start to build credibility in this way, you will make people believe. You'll start with yourself and move on to your jury of customers, clients, investors, team members, and loved ones. And once they believe, they'll start advocating as well.

Turning Adversaries into Advocates

You advocate every day. If you recommend a TV show, a restaurant, a podcast, or a book, you're advocating for that thing. Now consider why. Chances are, you believe in that thing. You believe that other people will like it. And because you believe, you have the enthusiasm and the motivation to put yourself on the line for it. You believe so strongly that you want to share it. You've become an advocate.

When companies study net promoter scores (a gauge of customer loyalty), they're trying to predict which customers will become advocates for them. When real estate agents count on referral business, they're counting on prior clients advocating for them. When I collect testimonials from my coaching clients, those clients become my advocates. (Good thing I've taught them so well!)

When people find something they believe in, they want to share it. That is why it's possible to turn almost anyone into an advocate. In the introduction to this book I shared the story of the patient who sued the doctor and then referred her loved ones to that same doctor. She went from an adversary to an advocate, and she did so because she came to believe the doctor. Using the tools of an advocate, that doctor was able to build his credibility. He advocated for himself, and then she joined him.

That's why advocates win. They're not alone. When you use the tools in this book to become a strong advocate for yourself, your business, and your ideas, you will build credibility. Others will come to believe, and then they'll advocate for you, too. And that's how you get success greater than you've ever imagined. When others advocate for you, you get referral business. You boost your net promoter score, get more social media shares, grow your podcast, and build a strong family. When you turn the people around you into your advocates, the wins start coming fast and furious.

Good advocates can even turn adversaries into advocates, using credibility as the greatest tool.

Own Your Bad Stuff

In the Evidence chapter, you will learn about knowing all the evidence, including that which could hurt you. When it comes to building credibility, you have to be willing to know your own bad stuff and own it. That means owning that you aren't perfect.

It means owning that you are human. And it means owning your tears when they're real. I learned that, once again, in the courtroom.

Three years before I wrote this book, I had a case that involved a surgeon who had performed a surgery that resulted in a nerve injury. It was a straightforward, medically simple case, and I'd defended many like it. The patient's injury was a slight limp, which is relatively minor compared to many of my other cases. We had a very strong medical defense and a great expert. But the surgeon was arrogant. In most of my cases there are two years of discovery between when a case is filed and when it goes to trial. In the two years leading up to this case, I worked hard with the surgeon to help him learn and use the tools of a trial lawyer. We worked on using words that would resonate with the jury. I gave him ways to consider seeing things from the jury's perspective. We practiced questions and answers, and in the process worked on his reception and presentation skills. And yet, I knew we still had a problem. He was just arrogant and not willing or able to change.

The night before his testimony we were still prepping. Normally, I meet with doctors the weekend before their testimony and encourage them to focus on clarity and sleep the night before they testify. But this doctor wanted to do things his way, so it was eleven o'clock on the Wednesday night of the second week of trial and we were prepping.

"I think you'll be fine. I need to go home and work on my motion for a nonsuit that I have to argue in the morning. Try to get some sleep."

"Heather."

I looked up from packing my trial bag to see what he wanted.

"Should I cry?"

He smirked as he asked the question, and my hopes sank.

"No, Doctor, I don't think you should cry. I think the jury will know that the tears aren't real, and they'll hate you for it."

The next day, he testified. He cried. And we lost that case. In fact, the jury gave an award that was many times higher than you'd expect in that type of case.

He'd used the tools I gave him, but in this case, poorly. He'd manipulated them and ruined his credibility. The tears weren't real. That showed, and he lost spectacularly.

But tears aren't always bad. All the tools you have just learned about can be used to make your jury, whether Inner or Outer, believe. A young female obstetrician I was representing used my tools. She'd delivered a mother's twins, and one of the babies died. It was a tragic, catastrophic case. The medicine was complicated. Reading fetal monitoring strips is tough for anyone. It took me years to really start to grasp them. Explaining them to the jury is enormously difficult. But we knew that the doctor had done all she could, even if that was going to be a challenge to make the jury understand.

On the afternoon before her testimony I told the doctor to go home, get some sleep, and spend time with her family. I assured her that she was ready and that she'd be a wonderful witness. She made it clear that she had faith in me but doubted herself.

That night I got a phone call from the doctor. We talked about the procedure of her testimony, walking to the witness stand, asking for water.

"Heather, what if I cry?"

Her voice shook as she asked the question.

"Doctor, it's okay if you cry. If you cry it will be real, and the jury will know that it's real. They'll understand and they might even love you for it."

The next day she testified. She cried, almost imperceptibly. And we won the case.

The juries in both cases saw through the doctors. When the first doctor cried, they saw it wasn't real, and he lost their credibility. When the second doctor cried, they saw it was real, and she built her credibility. Don't be afraid to cry. Do be afraid to lose your credibility.

Precedent

I had to learn about building credibility myself as well. Starting a business is a real opportunity to learn about yourself and how far you're willing to go to maintain your credibility.

I was building an online course as a companion to this book. In order to grow my audience, I'd created Facebook ads that directed anyone interested to a mini-course. If they liked the smaller version of the course, they'd buy the full course. Technology isn't my strong suit, so I hired someone to help me program the back-end. And then I woke up one day to find that people were signing up for the mini-course and not receiving it. I had three emails from irate potential customers.

My first inclination was to cry or hide. I'd lost credibility with these three women before I'd even started, and that bothered me immensely. I'd promised a mini-course and hadn't kept that promise. I'd set the expectation that they'd get an email with the first lesson contained therein. They did not. But after some self-coaching, I realized I had but one option: own it.

I reached out to the three women who didn't get what they'd expected. I explained what happened (as best as I understood it). I apologized and sent them all the seven day mini-course, in one email, to ensure they'd received it. I offered each a free one-hour coaching session. I owned my mistake. And the women appreciated it. They accepted my apology and the free session. Two of the three then signed up for one-on-one coaching. I think if I'd simply had my assistant send them an email, they'd never have bought from me—not the course and not personal coaching. By owning it, I'd changed our relationship and built my credibility. In doing so, I created clients that I hope to serve for a long time.

Summary of the Case: Credibility

1. *You can't advocate until you believe.* It's almost impossible to make other people believe in something you don't. When I try my cases, I have to find a theory of the case that I believe before I can try to make the jury believe. You have to believe in yourself and your story before you can make your jury believe as

well. Persuade your Inner Jury, and the Outer Jury becomes a whole lot easier.

2. *People are always going to believe in something.* It may as well be you. Everyone is looking for something to believe in. Why not you? Just as we often look to someone outside of us to advocate for us, we also often look outside of us for something to believe in. But why give your belief away so freely? Believe in yourself first and foremost. That helps you make others believe as well.

3. *Be sure to leave an advocate behind.* Everywhere you go and everything you do, you're advocating. You always have the chance to turn your Outer Jury into your advocates. In the courtroom, that's imperative. I want to have as many members of the jury as I can arguing for my client and my win when they deliberate. I need as many advocates as I can get. I work to persuade my jurors to believe in me and my case so strongly that they feel compelled to advocate. You want to do the same with your Outer Jury.

Chapter 6
Evidence

*Truth is the story the jury chooses based
on the evidence you present.*

What's true? Whatever they believe. And you make them believe
with evidence.

Evidence is another tool of a trial attorney. Anything and
everything can be evidence, so using evidence allows you to be
creative. Wake up in the morning and your alarm time could
be evidence of motivation or laziness. Do you hit snooze? More
evidence. If you leave your coffee cup in the sink it could be
evidence that you're lazy, messy, or inconsiderate. Or it could be
evidence that you're in a rush. Sit down at your desk and immediately go to Facebook. That could be evidence that you're easily
distracted. Or it could be evidence that it's your birthday. Start
your workday and every piece of data, every email, every phone
call, and every report is a piece of evidence. Anything you could
possibly use to prove your story is evidence. Evidence is data,

research, stories, and testimonials. It's videos, pictures, audio, and statistics.

Remember our maxim that facts tell and stories sell but advocates win? Your facts are your evidence, and then you tell stories about that evidence. It's the evidence you choose and the way you share it that allows you to advocate. When there are competing stories, both stories are often based upon the same evidence. It's how you use it that counts.

Early in my career I had a friend who learned about winning, and losing, with evidence the hard way.

He was so excited he was practically vibrating. My friend was going to try his first case on his own, and he'd been bragging about it for weeks. It's a big deal for a trial attorney to have his first case to try. After years as a second-chair attorney, carrying bags and indexing exhibits, when we finally get the chance to stand before a jury, present our evidence, and argue our case, we celebrate the opportunity.

My friend's case was a general liability case—a slip-and-fall. The plaintiff had sued an event venue claiming he'd fallen at the venue and slipped a disc. He said the person cleaning the venue left a puddle of water on the floor, and there was no sign or warning. He claimed he'd been unable to return to work or do his activities of daily life since the fall. He said he could barely walk and his wife had to do all of the household chores he used to do. My friend was defending the venue, and their defense was that there wasn't a puddle and the plaintiff had just slipped. But they also claimed the plaintiff was overstating his damages. In other words, they said he was faking.

The reason my friend was so excited on this particular day was that they were about a week away from trial and his private investigator had just called him with news. The investigator had been hired to do surveillance on the plaintiff, and he'd hit the jackpot.

My friend could barely contain himself as he told me the details ahead of trial.

"So, he sees Mr. M [the plaintiff] leave his house, walking just fine, but he doesn't have time to get a video of it because he's walking too fast. My guy follows him, and Mr. M drives to a nearby park. Then Mr. M gets out of his car with a basketball in his hands, walks to the public court, and plays a game of pickup basketball!" he told me.

"He says he can't even walk, and he played basketball for over two hours! I watched the video, Heather—this wasn't a game of HORSE. This was grown men, pushing and fighting to win. My guy was running, jostling, and fouling like crazy. I can't believe what a liar this guy is. And I can't wait to show it to the jury," my friend said.

"This sounds amazing. I can't wait to hear how it plays out in front of the jury. Good luck and call me after," I said. "I want to hear everything."

Days later my friend called, but I almost didn't recognize him. His voice was despondent, and his tone low. I asked what was wrong.

"You're not going to believe what happened. I can't believe it. You're not going to believe it."

I waited, in silence, for him to continue. He told me what happened.

Mr. M testified, and the jury liked him. It took him thirty minutes to get up to the stand, and he grimaced and moaned like a loon the whole way. My friend said, "I loved it, because I knew all of those shenanigans were going to make him look even worse once the jury saw the tape." He also told me, "I didn't pay a ton of attention to his testimony, to be honest, because I knew that all I needed to do in my cross was to play the tape."

Then it came time for cross-exam. "I set him up perfectly. 'You said you can't walk? How far can you walk? You said you can't work? Why not?'" My friend thought he had laid the best trap ever. Then once the man told the jury that he was practically on his deathbed, my friend played the video.

"Sir, then how do you explain this video?"

I was dying to hear the witness's explanation.

"That's my twin brother."

Well, that was a problem.

I shudder to this day to think how my friend felt at that moment. What do you do? How do you recover? My friend didn't do much. He had no other questions planned and didn't have a follow-up question for such an unexpected answer. He fussed with his papers, asked a few more questions, and practically waved a white flag. That case was closed.

What a lesson.

My friend only practiced trial law for a short time after that and then decided to go work as general counsel in a corporation where he wouldn't have to cross-examine twins. I went on to try cases for another twenty-plus years. The two lessons I learned from my friend's experience helped me win most of those cases, and it will help you advocate for yourself and your ideas as well.

First, it reminded me to never rely on *just one piece of evidence.* You never know when it will let you down. My friend didn't prepare for other angles. He thought his one piece of evidence was so good that he didn't have to question Mr. M about his medical records or his deposition. He was so focused on this one thing that he had nothing to fall back on when that one thing blew up in his face.

Second, this case with my friend inspired me to develop my Win/Lose/Weird Process, which has changed my life and those of both the clients I coach and those I represented. It is a way of analyzing every piece of evidence. First you ask, "How could this help me win?" In the case of my friend and the twin, that was obvious. He saw that the surveillance tape could easily win the case for him in a dramatic and easy way, so he stopped there. But if he had gone on to the next step, he would have been in a much better position in the courtroom that day. The next step is to ask, "How could this help me lose?" It's important to ask this question about every piece of evidence, even those things that seem like slam dunks.

My friend hadn't analyzed the evidence as well as he could have. At his deposition, Mr. M had told my friend that *he had a brother*. It didn't seem relevant at the time, so my friend didn't explore it further. Whoops. He didn't ask how old the brother was or where he lived. Had he asked those two questions, he might have realized that Mr. M had a twin. Had he looked at how this evidence could make him lose, he might have considered that the brother might have been a twin. Then he could have done a little more investigation before the trial and not been surprised by this new piece of evidence.

In addition, my friend didn't consider the *weird*. It's weird that Mr. M had a twin brother who was an identical twin, drove a similar car, and lived with Mr. M. In fact, it seems a little too weird, don't you think? Even all these years later, I'm not convinced that it was Mr. M's twin playing basketball. I think Mr.

M might have just been quick on his feet (on cross, not in basketball) and he caught my friend unprepared and unaware. But if my friend had considered the weird, he may have had a different outcome. At the very least, he'd have had something to say.

These two lessons apply broadly in life. Whether you're persuading your Inner Jury or your Outer Jury, you need evidence. And you don't want to rely on just one piece of evidence to win your client, your customer, your sale, or the support of your team. If you think you have the best story ever, use it. But be willing to also present another testimonial and another piece of research. When you believe that the data you've found makes your offer a no-brainer, consider that other brains may differ. Be ready with more. Even when you think you have one winning piece of evidence, keep looking. You want to play with the evidence until you know it all, inside and out, including the opposing side of your argument. Know how your evidence fits into your story and how it fits into any competing stories. Every minute you spend playing with evidence helps you better know and understand what you're advocating for and the circumstances that surround it. Knowing all the evidence also helps you think on your feet when things come up, like they did for my friend.

Playing with the Evidence

Playing with the evidence is the first step in applying the Win/Lose/Weird Process. The people I coach tell me that the thing they like and hate the most is when I tell them to play with the evidence. They like it because it leads to wins. They hate it because it isn't easy. It can be hard, boring, monotonous, and thankless work. But when you're faced with a Mr. M, you'll be glad you did it.

To play with evidence, first collect your *body of evidence*. That's all the evidence you can use to support whatever it is you're asking for. If you're asking yourself whether you should move to another apartment, your evidence is going to be different than if you're asking investors for money. If you're asking your spouse for better boundaries, your evidence is going to be different than if you're asking a customer to buy from you or an investor to give you seed money. But no matter what you're asking for, there's always evidence to support the request.

Imagine you're trying to sell your services as a graphic artist. You approach a potential client who's never heard of you or seen your work. In order to sell him, you use your evidence to prove your value. You show him pictures of the campaigns you've done for other clients. You share testimonials from those clients about how easy it was to work with you and how thrilled they were with the results. You've created a video montage of all your work, set to music. You have a graph that shows the return on investment (ROI) various clients have seen from your services. All this is evidence. No matter what you do or what you want, evidence is the key to providing yourself and your value to your juries, both **Inner and Outer**.

Here's a thorough, though not exhaustive, list of all the evidence available for the various life situations you'll face:

Data
Statistics
ROI values
Research

Comparisons

Features

Stories

Props

Testimony from clients

Testimony from influencers

Testimony from employees

Experiences

Videos

Pictures

Before-and-after visuals

Audio

Historical behavior

Feelings

Collect it all, leaving no stone unturned and no evidence unexamined. Don't choose not to list something because you don't like it or don't think it's strong enough. Don't censor yourself at all. At this point you're not making any judgments. You're just making a list including everything you have available to you.

Let's use another practical life example. Imagine you want to convince yourself that you're capable of running a marathon. You might look at data on how many miles you need to run in a week in order to train for one. And you could look at statistics on how many people like you have run marathons in the past. You'd want to collect stories of when you'd done hard physical things in the past, and perhaps a medal you had from a prior race. If you could find video or pictures of yourself running, that's more evidence. You'd also want to collect stories of when you quit running when your knees started hurting, and input from past coaches who felt you didn't have the drive to race competitively. Collect all the evidence that supports or challenges whether you can run a marathon.

Your marathon list might look something like this:

Data: You've run thirty miles a week for the past six weeks.

Statistics: Seventy percent of people who run marathons have similar running experience to you.

Stories: Your friends have run marathons and loved their experiences.

Experience: You've been able to finish long races without any issues.

Video/Pictures: You have shots and videos of you running in the past.

Some of my clients struggle with making a list of evidence because they're afraid they'll never stop collecting it. These tend to be my type A overachievers who want to make sure they have everything available. I tell them to do what I do in my cases. I make sure I know everything about every piece of evidence that's currently available to both sides. And then I stop. Otherwise I could be researching and exploring things outside the case and wasting the precious time I could otherwise spend weighing the evidence. Know what you need to know better than anyone else—but only as it pertains to the case at hand. In the case of the marathon list, that means you don't need to research the last woman to run a marathon, her time, and her age. In the graphic artist sales example, you don't need to know about every other graphic artist in the world, just the one you're in competition with. Collect enough evidence to feel confident and prepared.

Win/Lose/Weird Process

Once you've made your list, it is time to weigh it with the WLW Process. Look at each piece of evidence one at a time, and weigh all the ways that piece of evidence can help you win. Write it down. For my friend, writing down ways that the video of Mr. M could help his case would have been easy. Mr. M would lose credibility with the jury. He'd look like a fool and a liar.

Then also write down how each piece of evidence could make you lose. For example, the jury could have liked Mr. M so much that they could have been angry at my friend for having hired an investigator to hide in the woods and take pictures of him. That's always a very real possibility with surveillance (and a reason I avoided it in my legal practice). Consider all the ways that the perfect piece of evidence might not be so perfect.

Focusing on the *lose* can be tough for some people. I had a client who used to call me Chicken Little. He said that when we were prepping, I was always pointing out the bad parts of the case. He didn't like it. He didn't want to look at how we could lose. But you can't win until you see how you could lose. You have to know the evidence that could hurt you so you can avoid the pain. I'd much rather have my client walking away from a trial saying, "You prepared me for so many things they didn't ask," than "I had no idea that was coming."

Call me Chicken Little as long as you also call me the winner.

You need to be willing to see the bad stuff, too. Some of my clients initially worry that it will be a blow to their self-confidence, but then, once we've worked together, it becomes clear the opposite is true. When you know you've faced the worst and you can face it again, your confidence soars. You're ready for anything. That makes for a formidable advocate.

Finally, write down all the weird things that could happen with that piece of evidence. If my friend had done this step he might have come up with the possibility of a twin. That's weird, but I've had lots of weird things happen in trials. Heart attacks in the courtroom, uteruses in jars, and drug deals during breaks all come to mind. You'll never anticipate the exact weird that will actually happen, but if you make room for it, you're going to be far more prepared for the actual weird when it occurs.

Now you've got your body of evidence. But you're not finished with the WLW Process, because you have to do it again. You take each piece of evidence and decide whether it's more of a winner or a loser. The evidence that is crowned the winner will be what to focus on when you advocate. You don't want to focus on the losers, obviously, but you do want to be prepared for them.

7X7W System

The next step is to take all the evidence and apply the 7X7W System. This system is what helps you to communicate your evidence to your jury. There's an old marketing concept that says you have to repeat something seven times in order for anyone to truly hear it. They say no one will be really aware of what you're saying about your product, and willing to buy it, until you've said it seven times. And it's true that repetition brings recognition. The more you see or hear something, the more familiar it is to you. Given the amount of content being thrown at us every day, I'd suspect that we might even need to hear things more than seven times in order to really recognize and remember them. So be sure to repeat yourself, whether you're advocating to your Inner Jury or your jury of clients/customers.

In trial, it's not enough to tell the jury something once. To be sure, lawyers must repeat the good evidence so that everyone remembers it and is able to repeat it to the other jurors during deliberations (without driving the jury crazy). And that's a very fine line. Jurors may need to hear a message seven times, but that doesn't mean they want to. It's more likely they roll their eyes, nudge each other, and sigh loudly when an attorney repeats the message on time five or six. That's where the 7W comes in. In the courtroom, I did my best to share the evidence with the jury seven times and in as many ways as possible. I used a medical record, my opening statement, my doctor's testimony, my expert's testimony, a demonstration before the jury, a nurse's testimony, and a PowerPoint we'd created. That's seven. I could have also worked to get an opposing witness to say it on cross-examination. Maybe, in a perfect world, I'd find a way to take the language the judge uses in her instructions and repeat it in such a way that it speaks to that piece of evidence.

Be creative.

I coach my clients to communicate their good evidence seven times and seven ways as well. That means taking all your good evidence that supports your argument and being creative about how you share it. You could use a graph and a story. Then you could email it, share it in a webinar, put it in a video, and share it by phone. Ideally, you have other people sharing it for you as well. They become your advocates. Social media and social proof are great ways to be sure your message is being repeated and hopefully remembered.

As I mentioned at the start of this chapter, my clients both hate and love all that we do to play with the evidence. The 7X7W System can be boring and frustrating, and feel impossible at times. It's not always easy to come up with another way to communicate the evidence. But it is also the key to many of my clients' greatest wins. First, it allows them to know the evidence better than anyone else. And second, and perhaps most important, it allows them to communicate the evidence in a way that will best resonate with their particular jury. When you have a jury that likes stories, use a story. Your jury is made up of scientists or researchers? Use research. You get to combine the evidence with perspective and really drive your point home.

Perspective and Evidence: Inner Jury

When you're playing with the evidence, keep in mind that there's always another perspective. One of the greatest and most life-changing lessons I've learned from being a trial attorney is that there's often no such thing as the truth. Instead, there's what you choose to believe. In my cases there were always two stories—the patient's story and the doctor's story. Each witness steps up into the witness stand and swears or affirms that they will tell the truth. They each tell their story to the jury, using the exact same evidence in different ways. Those stories often contradict each other completely. Then the jury chooses which story is the truth. This has made it very clear to me that there are very few things we can say are "true." Most of the time the things we consider true are simply what we choose to believe. Once you choose to believe something, you find evidence to support it. You work to make it true. And your job as an advocate is to make them believe you. You do it with evidence.

Here's an example from my life. I like sunglasses—a lot. My sunglass collection is extensive, and my mum, nieces, sister, and friends all have the sunglasses that no longer suit me or suit them better. While I was writing this book, I bought a new pair of sunglasses from Tiffany. They were black, with Tiffany blue inside, and I loved them.

It was during the pandemic, and I wanted to get antibody testing to see whether living in New York had exposed me to COVID. I had an appointment to get tested, but I was late. I ran out of the house with my wallet, my phone, and AirPods, and my sunglasses tucked into the collar of my shirt. Halfway to the doctor's office I heard something drop. When I felt my pockets, my phone and AirPods were there. I hurried on. About a block away from the doctor's I realized what had happened. I'd dropped my sunglasses.

I doubled back to my apartment looking for the glasses. They were nowhere to be found. I retraced my steps to the doctor's, now very late, but still no sunglasses. On the walk back to my apartment (my second walk back) I once again combed the street. They were gone.

When I got home, I berated myself for hours. I told my Inner Jury the story that I was careless, impatient, and reckless. I told her that I didn't deserve to have nice things, that I was irresponsible with my stuff, and that I was always hurried and harried. That story had me feeling disappointed in myself, frustrated, and angry. My sessions with my coaching clients didn't go very well that day. My energy was terrible.

Finally, I realized that I needed another story for my Inner Jury. I found a story that I could believe. In this story, a woman was walking down the street moments after me when she looked down and saw these brand-new, gorgeous Tiffany glasses. She picked them up and looked around to see to whom they belonged. She even asked some people passing by if they belonged to them. When she couldn't find the owner, she took them home and washed them off. She slipped them on, and they felt magical. The glasses made her feel classy, special, and beautiful. She showed them to her family, and her daughters tried them on. Now every time that woman wears those sunglasses, she feels magical.

I found evidence to support that story. The glasses were gone. I'd checked the route I'd taken twice. And since they were clearly women's glasses it would have been a woman who would have picked them up. I also had friends who had found sunglasses before, cleaned them up, and worn them for years. All this evidence allowed my Inner Jury to believe this story. And that belief made me happy and even delighted at the idea that this woman was enjoying the sunglasses even more than I had.

Be Sure to Leave an Advocate Behind: Outer Jury

You'll find that when you become a strong advocate for yourself and your ideas, people around you will start supporting you as well. They'll sing your praises, tell others to hire you, or refer you for work. These people will believe in you so strongly that they want to share their enthusiasm. What a gift! That means it is your job to help them give that gift to you. Make it easy for them.

The best way to leave an advocate behind is to leave them with evidence to help them advocate.

In the courtroom, when the trial is over and all the lawyers have given their closings, the judge then "charges" the jury. She reads them all the law that applies to the case, and then the jurors go back into the deliberation room, usually with nothing more than their memories to help them come to a verdict. That's when the lawyers start pacing. If you've read my book *The Elegant Warrior*, you know that this time is pure hell for the lawyers. Some lawyers go back to their offices, but I always stayed in City Hall so that I knew I'd be close by if and when the jury called.

Sometimes the jury would ask to have testimony read back to them. Other times they might have asked to see a certain exhibit or piece of evidence. When the jury asked for a piece of evidence that I'd focused on, I took that as a good sign. It meant that at least one juror back there heard me, and my 7X7W made the evidence more memorable. I'd gotten through to them. It meant that someone wanted to use that exhibit, and my assumption was that they were using it to advocate for my client and me. I always wanted to leave an advocate behind, and giving them evidence that helped them to advocate for me was part of my job.

You want to leave an advocate behind as well, so create exhibits: slides, pictures, and whatever is relevant for the matter at hand. Some examples include:

- Create a chart for the chores in your house so your kids can advocate for the plan even when you're not in the room.
- Tell a story that your partner will always remember when he's talking to his mother and she is about to cross a boundary.
- Email a follow-up with bullets to your team after a call to get their buy-in.
- Before you give a presentation, email a memo or a slide deck with pictures of what you intend to explain or graphs of the data you'll use.

Give people tangible evidence to help them support you. They will be better advocates if they have it.

Precedent

A woman I coach was giving a huge presentation at work—that's why she reached out to me to work with her. There was a project up for grabs, and she was vying to lead it. She had a number of competitors for the spot. When we first began working together, she thought she wanted to work solely on Presentation. And while we did hone her body language, tone of voice, and energy, we also collected Evidence.

She'd run a similar project in the past—that was one piece of evidence. She had already come up with some ideas for the project—more evidence. Her colleagues supported her promotion to this role—even more evidence. We made a deck showing all the evidence that demonstrated she was the best person for the job. And she sent it to her managers (who would decide who got the project) before her presentation. This allowed the decision-makers to have some context and some information when she presented. It also allowed my client to leave advocates behind and to give them evidence that would help.

During her presentation, she referred to her evidence. Her presentation was highly interactive, and she called me afterwards, shocked that the managers had so many questions and so much feedback. She called me again, a week later, to tell me the project was hers. She used her Evidence to prove her case. And she won.

Summary of the Case: Evidence

1. *You have your evidence.* Collect it. Many of my coaching clients don't recognize that they have evidence right away. They haven't come to the realization that everything is evidence to support or challenge the story they want to tell. Once you make this realization, you can start using your evidence to your advantage.

2. *The Win/Lose/Weird Process and the 7X7W System work.* Work them, repeatedly, and in detail.
3. *Truth is nothing but a story with the evidence on its side.* Stop seeing truth as so black and white. Recognize that most of the time truth is subjective and that you can make it work for you.

Chapter 7
Reception

It's better to receive than to present.

When you learn to receive, you're on your way to getting everything that you want. Reception—the way you listen, sense, and read another person—is critically important to advocating to win.

I've been good at reading a room since I was a child. I could sense when my parents were in bad moods and knew when to avoid them. I always felt when other children were hurting even if they didn't specifically say so. As I got older and got my degree in psychology, I felt a lot of what people were feeling even if they didn't actually say it. Over time, I realized that I was tuning into people on a level that we don't often talk about, and when we do it is in a way many consider a little *out there*. I studied things like chakras, auras, and energy fields. I believe we all have a subtle energy field that can be sensed and influenced, but I also believe that some of that energy field is more concrete. I always knew that a person's tone of voice was an important way to sense her emotion and that facial expressions and body language could tell me more than words would in some instances. I used all these inputs as ways to read people as I studied psychology.

But when I chose to become a trial lawyer, I had no idea that the ability to sense people's frequency could serve me. Law seemed very black and white from the outside. It's not. The courtroom is ultimately just another room filled with people. Those people have their energies, their tones of voice, their body language, and their facial expressions, too. The ability to sense those energies has helped me to read a witness, understand a doctor, or sense a jury's confusion. I can use reception to help me win, and you can, too.

First, though, you have to be aware that you're receiving. Most of the time, people just aren't that aware. I had a case involving a very difficult patient's attorney. He was notorious for being angry, nasty, and combative. Lots of attorneys love making life terrible for opposing counsel, and he did. He loved to fight and strove to make things as difficult as possible for people on the other side. He made every case a nightmare, and his reputation as a nightmare preceded him. I'd been able to avoid him throughout most of my career. Then I was assigned a new case, and his name was on the complaint. I steeled myself for two years of swearing, yelling, and constant battle.

Attorneys like this guy love depositions. In court the judge is there to serve *as a judge*. They keep things under control. I often think of judges as parents, moderating quarrels between hyperactive children. And when one of those children is consistently aggressive, mean, and even dangerous, the judge figures it out quickly. In court, this attorney was relatively controlled. He still yelled, but less loud. He still insulted, but less profanely. But during depositions, all bets were off. A deposition is an attorney's opportunity to ask all the questions he needs to ask of a party. All the attorneys are there, along with the witness and the court reporter. But no judge. There's no one to calm things down when they get heated. I've had one deposition where the attorneys almost came to blows. I've seen others where the attorneys swore like sailors. I knew that this attorney loved the idea that one or the other might happen.

I had another problem with this specific case: my doctor. My doctor was also quite volatile. I'd represented him before, and he was an aggressive defendant. He wanted every case thrown out the minute it was filed, and when I told him the law just doesn't work that way, he rebelled. He told me to make every day as difficult for the opposing attorney as possible. This doctor was looking for a fight just as much as the other attorney was. In our prior case, I'd asked the doctor to think of the deposition differently. I wanted him to see it from another perspective. Rather than seeing it as a fight with opposing counsel, I asked him to see it as the chance to speak to the jury. When cases go to trial, the deposition (which is often videotaped) can be played for the jury. I asked him to see this not as a time to attack the attorney but rather to embrace the jury. I begged him to try it my way for this one deposition. And he did. He was charming, funny, and likable. In fact, he was so likable that the plaintiff's attorney dropped the case a few weeks later. He'd filed the case because he heard the doctor was an ogre and he was counting on the jury hating him. He dropped it not because he liked the doctor, but because he knew the jury would. This was good because the doctor learned the power of perspective and presentation. And I hoped he'd remember it in this case.

But I was about to learn a little more about reception.

My preparation for this specific deposition was more than just knowing the medical records inside and out. I also had to engage in a ton of self-talk. I knew that when the opposing attorney went hard, I'd have to soften. When he yelled, I'd have to go quiet. When he went full-on warrior, I'd have to go full-on elegance. Because I knew that the minute my doctor sensed my frustration, anger, or dislike, I'd lose him. I knew my doctor was very receptive to energy in a room, even if he didn't know it. I knew the best way to control his testimony was to control my energy.

Years of meditation, mindfulness, and journaling have made me good at this. I'm usually able to find that space: that moment between reacting and responding. And I found it, again and again, during this deposition. Opposing counsel would get angry, and I'd get calm. He'd be snide, and I'd be smiling. He insulted, and I inhaled and exhaled. I acquiesced where I could to keep things moving. I saw that co-defense counsel were looking at me funny. There were two other defendants in the case, and they were represented by men who had fought like tigers during their clients' depositions. In fact, one deposition had to be ended because of the fighting, and that attorney's client, another doctor, had to take another day off from his patient care and come back for another stressful deposition. I didn't want that for my doctor. As long as I was objecting appropriately and protecting my client, I'd let opposing counsel do his thing.

And it worked. The more my doctor and I were charming, the more opposing counsel was charmed. The more we responded to negative with positive, the closer we came to a middle ground.

It was going so well that I sacrificed myself to keep the deposition moving forward, but that proved to be a clever strategy.

At 9:00 a.m. when we started, I'd said I had to end the deposition at 3:00 p.m. because I had to get back to NYC to receive an award that night. But by one o'clock I knew we wouldn't be done, and I knew I didn't want my doctor to have to come back another day. During our lunch break, the doctor stepped outside to take a call. I let the other attorneys and the court reporter know I was going to miss the awards ceremony and finish the dep that day. And for some reason this set one of the co-defendant's attorneys off. I think he missed the conflict he was accustomed to.

"What?" he barked. "You said you were ending at 3:00 p.m. I'm not ready to question your guy. And I have a ton of questions for him. A ton. We're going to be here all night."

"Okay," I said. "Ask what you have to ask. We'll stay as long as it takes. And you have time to organize your questions."

The patient's attorney wasn't yet close to being done with his questions, so there was plenty of time for this attorney to get himself together.

"No! You said you were ending at 3:00 p.m. This is ridiculous."

His face was red, he was spitting in anger, and he was yelling. I don't know if he was upset because he saw that my doctor was doing better than his client had done. I don't know if he thought I was being too nice to opposing counsel.

I do know that he was losing it, and at that moment my doctor came back into the room. He looked around, and immediately his energy changed. I could see it happen. The way he held his body changed, like he was ready to charge. His eyes narrowed and his teeth bared a little.

"What's the problem?" he asked in a raised voice.

I pulled the doctor aside, and in as soothing a voice as I could muster I told him all that he needed to know.

"I'm not going to my thing tonight. You're doing great, and I want to get this over for you. That attorney was just annoyed that he has to be ready with questions for you today."

But the energy in the room had already impacted my client. His fists were clenched, and his eyes were bright with anger. His tone was full of animosity as he spat, "I will take him down! Does he know what I could say about his goddamn client? I will take him down!"

Holy moly.

All my hard work seemed to be going up in smoke. If my doctor went back into the deposition and faced opposing counsel giving off this kind of energy, the afternoon was not going to go well. I had to start back at square one. I took the doctor outside, and we walked around the block while I slowly and methodically talked to him about our plan and how well it was going. I watched his breathing slow and his eyes clear. His hands relaxed, and by the end of our short walk his charming smile returned to his face. We were able to get through the deposition without additional drama. And the co-defendant's attorney asked all the questions he wanted. He also ultimately lost the case. We won.

Energy impacts outcome, and ours led to a win.

That doctor didn't know it, but he was enormously sensitive to energy. He walked into a room, felt negative energy, and fed off it. Fortunately, I was able to sense what had happened and counter it.

You can learn to do the same—to receive others' energy consciously and curiously. And it could be the most powerful tool in your belt.

Receiving Yourself

If you can't tune into your own energy and your own tone, you'll never be able to read others'. Same for your Inner Jury. The way we influence, persuade, or convince our Inner Jury is with self-talk. But it's also with self-listening.

How?

Have you ever listened to yourself? Like me, you probably talk to yourself every day whether you realize it or not. Hopefully this book has so far made you more aware of the words you use when you talk to yourself and much more motivated to use your self-talk productively. Self-listening is a far more abstract idea. But if you can master it, you will be much more likely to persuade your Inner Jury to make the best choices, the ones that serve you and your dreams.

Those voices need to be *heard* before you can choose whether or not to believe them.

Start by listening to yourself. Be aware of the *way* you talk to yourself, and then wait for the responses. They may be something you hear and sound like another, fainter set of voices inside your head. But the response might also be a quickening of your pulse or a pain in your belly. It might be the sound of your heartbeat or your stomach growling. Listen to your body and then listen for your intuition. When you're very still, very conscious, and very lucky, you might even hear the whisper of intuition—your elegance—telling you what to do next.

In that deposition it was my ability to listen to myself that allowed me to know how to handle the doctor's rising energy. As soon as I felt my pulse quicken and my stomach drop, I knew I had to slow down. Then I had to listen to my inner voice of experience, of intuition, and of calm. I heard the inner voice telling me to choose to rise above. If I hadn't listened to myself, I likely would have joined him on that wave of anger and frustration. Together we would have ridden that wave to a likely crash. But by listening to myself, my body, and my inner voice I recognized that there was another way.

For some of you, receiving yourself will be realized through other feelings. You might feel trepidation, longing, or pure joy in response to some of your self-talk. Note that feeling and give it some attention. Don't rush through the moments when those feelings make themselves known. Think about your self-talk as a conversation. Those feelings are a response. Honor them. Learn from them. The more you listen (with your ears or with your whole body), the more your inner voice will have to tell you. And soon you may even start to do more listening than speaking.

Suddenly you'll just know when a relationship isn't right for you. You'll feel it. When a negative chorus of voices inside your head tries to tell you that this might be your last chance at love or you're being too picky, your Inner Jury won't be persuaded. You'll have learned to listen to your the more positive voice and believe it. You'll have built that foundation of credibility.

Meditation definitely helps. This doesn't mean you have to sit in a chair and purposefully meditate for twenty minutes. I do because that's what works for me. On days I don't meditate, I can't find myself. I can't receive the words, the energy, or the intuition that may be available because I haven't put myself in the habit of receiving. But for others, that kind of meditation makes the negative voices inside their head have a field day and they can't stand it. Even though the noise will quiet down if you give it enough time, these clients don't want to go through the discomfort. If meditation isn't your thing, find another way. Run. Play the piano. Draw, journal, or take a long bath.

I am not going to tell you that you must receive yourself in a particular way. I am telling you that you must receive yourself.

Receiving builds the foundation to make your Inner Jury believe the voices that want what's best for you.

Receiving Others

There are many ways you can receive others.

Listen

By far the most important way to receive is by listening. Learn to listen well and the other ways of receiving will often follow. Listening is the key to getting what you want. It's one of the most important skills that an advocate can have. *The best listener wins.* This is because listening means not only hearing what someone says, but also how they say it. It means understanding the message and the messenger. When you listen well you are present, receptive, and open. Master this skill and you'll master your jury.

Start with words. Simply listen to the message that's being shared with you. When I was a young lawyer, I'd prepare to take patients' depositions for hours and hours. I'd review all the pleadings, medical records, and written discovery. Then I'd write down all my questions by hand. I'd ask them out loud, crossing some off and combining others to pack a better punch. No one could have been more prepared than me. But all that work was for naught if I didn't listen to the answers. And early on, I didn't.

I'd get to the deposition, flushed with excitement that I even got to take a deposition and ready with my list. I'd ask the question and carefully check it off with my favorite pen. Then I'd move on to the next question, totally missing all the possibility the answer had within it.

Every word someone gives you is a gift to open or a bomb to disarm. But if you don't listen, you miss it. I missed a lot in those days. My questions were good and thorough, and gave the leads on my cases plenty to work with, but I missed the information that the witness gave me that I could follow up on. I'd left my curiosity behind in that conference room, and I was just worried about myself. How was I asking the questions? Did the other, more experienced attorneys think I was smart? I was focused on me and not the answers.

Late in my career, when I took a deposition, I did just as much preparation. I read all the records, pleadings, and deps. But I stopped writing down questions. I started just asking and listening. And getting so much more information. I followed up on each idea, each allegation, and each inference. I didn't assume anything.

You can do the same. When you're preparing for a negotiation or a request, prepare like crazy. Examine all the evidence. Then when it comes time for the conversation itself, believe in yourself. Believe in the work you've done and the preparation that has allowed you all the evidence you need. Let that belief lead to the trust and confidence that you won't miss a thing if you don't look at your pad. Because you might miss many things if you don't listen. Listen to the words that others use. Be curious and ask yourself why they chose those words. As you now know, every word matters, and that's just as true when you're on the receiving end of words as on the giving end.

But don't just listen to the words. Also really tune in to the tone of the speaker. I'm a little obsessed with tone of voice, and I love to review the research on it. For example, did you know a woman can tell whether a man is cheating on her by his tone of voice?[15] That could be a very valuable skill in the right situation. But, most importantly, when it comes to advocating, I've also learned you can tell more about a person's emotion from his tone of voice than from all the other senses combined.[16] You want to know whether someone is upset by what you're asking for? Listen to tone. Want to know if your negotiation style is working with your boss? Tone tells you.

Reading tone through listening is a skill that improves with practice. In the early days of my workshops I did a lot of work with call center employees. I'd do an exercise where they'd wear blindfolds and try to discern a caller's emotion by their tone of voice. Not only did they almost always get it right, but they also thought it was moronic that this was even a thing. They clearly thought anyone could do what they were doing. But everyone couldn't. I've done similar exercises with CEOs and surgeons who were less skilled at reading tone of voice. The more you do this, the better you get. And the better you get, the more you get…what you want.

---

[15] Susan Hughes and Marissa Harrison, "Your Cheatin' Voice Will Tell on You: Detection of Past Infidelity from Voice," *Evolutionary Psychology* 15, issue 2 (June 2017).

[16] Michael Kraus, "Voice-Only Communication Enhances Empathic Accuracy," *American Psychologist* 72, no. 7 (2017): 644–654.

Practicing this skill also builds confidence. When you know you can read someone, you're willing to take little risks. You know you can be a little more aggressive in your ask, and then back down a little if the tone of your counterpart's voice tells you to. You can take more chances, secure in your ability to use tone to make small corrections before big ones are necessary.

Finally, when you're a good listener, you make the people around you better speakers. When you're an active, engaged listener, the speaker will give you more information that is relevant and detailed. If you're negotiating for a raise or an opportunity, relevant and detailed information is information you want.

Listen with your all your energy attuned to what you are hearing. Listen with your energy attuned to the speaker. You'll see benefits immediately.

And it's especially powerful to be a good listener when you're communicating on video. I'm writing this book during the 2020 COVID-19 epidemic, and the world is changing. We're communicating almost completely via video, and that changes the way we communicate. People often don't feel listened to or heard on a video. Change that and you're at a huge advantage.

If you're advocating on video, start receiving by turning on your camera. I don't care if you don't look cute, and neither does the speaker. The speaker just wants to know that you're there and that you care. I believe every one of us wants to feel safe, smart, and special. When your speaker is talking to a blank screen, she doesn't feel safe. In fact, studies show that the primitive part of our brains don't feel at all safe on a video call.[17] It's because we

---

[17] Jeremy Bailenson, "Why Zoom Meetings Can Exhaust Us," *Wall Street Journal*, April 3, 2020, https://www.wsj.com/articles/

can't sense how far away others are, so we can't weigh how much of a threat they are. We also can't see each other's hands as easily, so we don't know whether someone has a weapon. No wonder a day full of video calls can leave some of us anxious.

Early in the COVID-19 pandemic, I attended a Zoom meeting where the entire group was men except for me. The vast majority of the group had their cameras off the whole time. Worse, those who had their cameras on were wandering around the house, taking phone calls, and clearly not paying attention. I purposefully looked directly into the camera the whole time. I wanted the speaker to feel heard and valued. After the meeting, the speaker reached out to thank me for my attention and my presence. He has since become one of my most successful clients.

Body Language and Facial Expressions

When you're using the tool of reception, you want to be aware of body language and facial expressions as well. There are whole books on these topics, and yet decoding body language and energy is much more difficult than one book or one lesson might imply. My best advice is to be aware. I've found that the more I've practiced receiving myself and tuning in to my own inner voice and inner energy, the better I am at reading others. I'm more grounded in my intuition and more able to see and feel what others are telling me with their bodies. It's also vital to interpret all body language and facial expressions in context. I am always cold, which means I almost always have my arms crossed if I'm not the one speaking. If you were to follow the experts' common

---

why-zoom-meetings-can-exhaust-us-11585953336.

advice, you'd read me as closed off, uninterested, and even hostile. Instead, I'm just cold. Before you jump to any conclusions about what your counterpart's body language is telling you, put it in context. And if you don't yet have any context on that person (you've never met before), then take my body language and facial expressions with a grain of salt. I encourage you to rely more on your ears, and what you're receiving from listening, than your eyes and reading bodies and faces. My clients do much better interpreting tone and words than they do with reading body language.

That doesn't mean to ignore the visual, though. You can use the visuals to mirror. Mirroring is when we move our bodies in a way similar to those around us. We do so in order to build rapport and be accepted, and most of the time we don't even realize we're doing it. Yawning is a great example of mirroring. When one person in a group yawns, others are sure to follow. Researchers believe this is a biological way to build rapport and to avoid aggression, but you can also use mirroring to build connections.

When you're receiving, you're more aware of the body language of the speaker. You can more easily and consciously mirror it. When they lean in, you lean in. When they make a surprised expression, allow your face to follow a little. Most of the time you'll want to do this naturally. But if you're aware of it you can use it to create better connections and better know your jury.

You also want to be discerning. During my deposition with the angry, aggressive attorney, I didn't want to mirror his body language. I had to be very aware and conscious of what I was receiving and how I was responding to it. Again, practice makes perfect. Practice receiving yourself and then practice receiving others. In time you'll be using what you receive in ways you can only imagine.

Put It All Together

The whole is the sum of its parts. Words, tone, energy, body language, and facial expressions are all important facets to receive in order to be the best advocate you can be. Each one on its own is helpful, and any one on its own could change your results when advocating.

One of my favorite studies demonstrates how much receiving has the potential to change everything.

The study involved a group of radiologists. Radiologists read X-rays, MRIs, and CAT scans. They don't often see the patient personally, and their only communication is with the doctor who ordered the study. Radiologists tend to have limited information about the patient. It's usually just the presenting complaint and the patient's demographics. But in this study, a group of radiologists were given the patients' CAT scans, plus the patients' pictures.[18] The radiologists read the studies, documenting what they found. They also documented incidental findings—those things that weren't relevant to the presenting complaint but could also be important. For example, on a hip study an incidental finding might be a problem with the colon. It might not be important to the hip surgeon, but it may be vitally important to the patient.

---

[18] Yehonatan N. Turner, Irith Hadas-Halpern, and David Raveh, "Patient Photos Spur Radiologist Empathy and Eye for Detail," Radiological Society of North America, press release, December 2, 2008.

Months later, that same group of radiologists was given the exact same studies, but they were not given the patients' pictures. Those radiologists missed 80 percent of the incidental findings! These doctors were not negligent. They were reading the studies as they'd been trained. But without the benefit of seeing the patient's face and receiving the input associated with that, they missed things. When you stop receiving all that is available to you, you miss things as well.

When you're getting ready to advocate, prepare. Choose your words, know your evidence, have your questions ready. But also prepare yourself to receive. Be present, open, and receptive. The more you receive, the more you get.

Precedent

One of my clients changed his entire business when he learned to listen. He is an entrepreneur, and he has a small but mighty team supporting his dream. And his dream could truly change the world. He has a plan to revolutionize health care in the United States, and I believe he will do it. His team believes as well. They are his best advocates. But it was only after he learned to listen that he tapped into the team's true potential.

His team had ideas. And during their weekly meetings, they'd share their ideas. But he wouldn't listen. When we first started working together, he wasn't even pretending that he was listening to his team. He'd go into the weekly meeting, share the information he needed to share, and then hop on his phone. After a short time of working together I encouraged him to try using these tools. As a result, he agreed to start leaving his phone in another room for his weekly work meetings. But he still wasn't listening.

That's when I shared one of my favorite tools for leaders. As each person on his team was speaking, I asked him to think of three questions to ask the speaker when she was done. This made him actually listen. He'd want to ask smart questions, so he'd pay attention. And then I had him ask the questions, both to show the team that he was listening and to show that curiosity was valued in the business.

The business changed dramatically. He got so much value out of what his team shared that he was able to delegate more and more of his work and focus on his superpowers. Together the team innovated twice as many solutions as when we first started working together. And his employees were more engaged and far less likely to leave. His churn rate decreased, and his entire team was happier.

Summary of the Case: Reception

1. *Tune into frequency.* Just like a radio can't pick up a signal unless it is tuned in to that signal, you have to tune in to your own frequency and those around you to pick up on all the messages that will help you advocate to win.

2. *The best listener wins.* When you listen, you get the information you're looking for, not only in what people say but also how they say it.

3. *Receive in context.* The better you know a person, the more you can trust your skills in receiving that person. You have to interpret everything you receive in the context of the sender.

Chapter 8
Presentation

When you communicate, you share perspectives. When you advocate, you change them.

When you communicate, you share perspectives, but when you advocate, you change them. That means you use more than words. You also use tone of voice, body language, and facial expression. That is also how we advocate. You need to use everything at your disposal when you're advocating for what you want, including presentation.

In the courtroom, doctors are often nervous to testify. Brilliant doctors tremble before they take the stand. The courtroom is not their world, and if they are there, they have a lot at stake. They know that cross-examination is going to be uncomfortable, to say the least, and that no matter how well I advocate for them they ultimately have to advocate for themselves. They have to use the tools I've given them—words, evidence, credibility, an awareness of their elegance, and the ability to see things through the jury's perspective—and persuade the jury. It's stressful.

I prepared my clients to testify with painstaking care, but on the stand they were on their own. I could object when the opposing attorney overstepped his bounds, but otherwise the witness held the weight of the case on his shoulders. On the days that my doctors were going to testify, they were often extremely nervous. And a nervous advocate is usually not the best advocate. I tried to distract them. I'd chat about weekend plans, the last movie I saw, or the last book they read. I'd look to anything that would distract my doctor from the challenge to come.

But one day, fifteen years into my career, I decided to share some insight about body language with my client before he testified. He was scheduled to testify right after the lunch break. Over the break he went outside to get fresh air, but he came back early and was pacing the courtroom. He came over to me as I put the final touches on my direct exam one last time. I decided to distract him by telling him about a study I'd just read. I'd always been interested in body language, tone of voice, and facial expression. I know that the energy of a speaker impacts the listener, and I use mine to my advantage when I can. One of the main reasons I majored in psychology and ultimately got my degree was because of one professor who taught us about paying attention to what a client's body was telling us as we listened to them speak. I loved everything to do with this topic. I'd just finished the book *Captivate* by Vanessa Van Edwards. In that book she talks about a study her team did where she asked volunteers to rate TED Talks. In her study she found that the least popular TED Talkers used an average of 272 hand gestures, while the most popular TED Talks used an average of 465 hand gestures.[19] I found this fascinating and worth mentioning to my client. He was interested and distracted from the trial at hand for a moment. My plan had worked! But then it came time for him to testify. That's when I realized my timing could have been better.

You can imagine what happened. When he took the stand to testify, my client conducted an orchestra. He waved his hands so much that he knocked the microphone off the lectern—twice. If the jury was looking at *my* body language, they were seeing me cringe and do everything I could not to motion for him to take it down a notch...or ten. When he came down off the stand and was done with his testimony, he was pleased as a peacock. He felt he had done well, and he had. The substance of his testimony was fabulous. But I wondered how the jury felt about his hand motions. I was beating myself up for sharing that study with my client right before he took the stand. Would they think he was grandiose, nervous, or clumsy?

Nope. They loved him.

At the end of the case they returned a verdict in his favor— we won. Not only that, they wanted to talk to the lawyers, and when we sat down with them, many of them said he was their favorite witness. This wasn't solely because of his hand motions. He used words, evidence, credibility, and questions to his benefit. And we'd worked for years, since the case was filed, on seeing things through the jury's perspective. I'd told him about reading the jury's body language and facial expressions and listening carefully to my tone, the judge's tone, and the tone of opposing

---

[19]   Vanessa Van Edwards and Brandon Vaughn, "5 Secrets of a Successful TED Talk," Science of People.

counsel. His presentation was another tool he used to earn that win. He'd advocated for himself extraordinarily well. His hands had helped.

Effective body language can lead to effective mirroring. I learned that in another trial. The doctor was one of the most charismatic witnesses I'd ever presented. I'd represented him a number of times before. He wasn't sued because he was a bad doctor, though. He was sued because he took on the patients that other doctors weren't willing to take. He operated on the patients who were high risk, and most of the time they got high return. But sometimes complications happened. Still, we never lost a case together. He's an exceptional advocate.

During this case, our third together, I knew how well he'd do. He'd spent weeks preparing for trial with me, choosing the right words to tell his story and seeing things through a patient's perspective to tell it in a way that would resonate. We practiced with questions, those he'd hear on direct exam and those he'd hear on cross. We'd talked about all the other tools of an advocate as well.

The patient in the case claimed that the doctor had made a mistake while performing a bunionectomy and that it led to her being unable to walk without a walker. She had been a very high-risk patient, and she also claimed she didn't know the risks. She said if she had known the risks, she wouldn't have had the surgery. I love when patients make that type of claim because most of the time they've signed a consent form that specifically lays out all the risks of the surgery. And in this case the doctor went even further and had his patients initial every paragraph of the form. She'd signed; she'd initialed. But she claimed that she'd signed the paper without reading it, and in my experience that testimony alone makes a patient lose credibility with the jury. But the doctor still had a job to do. He had to advocate for himself and tell the jury about his conversation with the patient about the risks.

He got on the stand, turned to the jury, and spoke to them. He saw things through their perspective and gave them analogies that applied to their lives. His body language was open and confident, and his tone was authoritative and kind. I could tell the jury loved him. But it also seemed the patient loved him. She was looking at him with wide, attentive eyes for the entirety of his testimony. And when he got to the part where he described his conversation with the patient, he looked right at her as he described their conversation.

"And I told her that given all of her other surgeries, and all of her medical problems, she was at increased risk for this surgery."

As he said the words and looked at the patient who sued him, he nodded his head. *And she looked at him, rapt with attention, and nodded her head right back at him.* She mirrored him perfectly. And in that moment I knew we'd won.

Once you've used words and evidence, questions and argument, and established your elegance and your credibility, presentation matters. It can't be your only tool, but it can be a very important one. And there are ways to use it to your advantage. As always, it starts with you.

Presenting to Your Inner Jury

You might think that this tool doesn't apply to your Inner Jury, but of course it does. The way you use your tone, facial expressions, and body language impacts your mood, your confidence, and your ability to advocate for yourself. You want to be sure to do it well.

Tone

Tone of voice is an often-untouched magic wand. As noted in the Reception chapter, you can learn more about a person's emotional state from his tone of voice than by body language and facial expressions combined. Over the years our training and conditioning have made us quite good at hiding our emotions physically, but we can't hide it from our tone of voice.

And you have a tone when you speak to yourself as well. I know I do it all the time. When I'm home alone and I drop a cup of hot tea I'll yell, "Come on, Heather!" When I'm suffering from a heartbreak I'll whisper, "You're going to be okay. You're okay." When I'm psyching myself up to advocate for myself I'll cheer, "You've got this!" Each of these statements is said with a definitive tone of voice, and thus they impact me differently.

I work with a number of mastermind groups made up of powerful women. One thing that has struck me time and time again is that when we talk about speaking to ourselves, almost every woman admits to yelling at herself. One will say her inner voice chides her for being late. Another will say her inner voice snaps when she forgets something or gets lost. But rarely do the women hear their inner voice urging them on, comforting them, or giving them praise. We need to change that, as quickly as possible. It takes awareness and practice.

Be aware when you're talking to yourself and be aware of the tone you're using. Don't use a tone with your inner voice that you wouldn't use with your outer voice. Don't speak to yourself in a tone you'd never use with your loved ones. The impact is greater than you might imagine, and this one thing could be a huge part of what's holding you back from being your own best advocate.

Facial Expressions

Here's some shocking news—your facial expressions impact your mood. Many of my clients think it's the other way around. They think when they're happy they smile and when they're sad they frown. But there's more to the story. Not only does your inner mood impact your outer presentation, your outer presentation impacts your inner mood. When you're smiling, you feel happier, and when you're frowning you feel worse.

There are great studies that prove this is true. One study took people with depression and injected Botox where frown lines normally appear. Botox freezes muscles and makes people unable to frown. These patients then reported that their depression had reduced by 27 percent. Another study showed that Botox reduced depression in patients with bipolar disorder and the depression came back when the Botox wore off![20] It seems that the less you frown, the less depressed you feel.

And the more you smile, the better you feel. In one study researchers asked participants to hold a pencil in their teeth in a way that mimics a genuine smile. Those participants were less stressed during a stressful task and showed faster physiological

[20] M. Axel Wolmer et al., "Facing Depression with Botulinum Toxin: A Randomized Control Trial," *Journal of Psychiatric Research* 46, issue 5 (May 2012).

recovery afterward.[21] When you fake a smile, your inner self believes it is true. And when you believe you're feeling good, you present completely differently. You're a better advocate.

Body Language

The way you hold yourself impacts how you feel. Stand up straight, you feel strong and proud. Slouch and close up, and you feel down and closed. You can test this for yourself, but research supports it. Some studies have shown that when you have bad posture you're more likely to be stressed out. In fact, when you sit up straight and proud your levels of cortisol (the stress hormone) could decrease by 20 percent.[22] And one researcher found that sitting in an upright position can improve mood and energy levels.

Your Inner Jury is always looking and always listening, and one of your jobs is to remove the marble to expose the angel, the elegance, inside. Sometimes the marble is the tone you habitually use when you talk to yourself or the posture you habitually use when you sit. We always want to start with our Inner Jury before we move on to our Outer Jury. You'll do so here as well, because

---

[21]   Tara L. Kraft and Sarah D. Pressman, "Grin and Bear It: The Influence of Manipulated Facial Expression on the Stress Response," *Psychological Science* 23, no. 11 (September 24, 2012): 1372–1378.

[22]   Amy J. C. Cuddy, Caroline A. Wilmuth, and Dana R. Carney, "The Benefit of Power Posing *Before* a High-Stakes Social Evaluation," Harvard Business School Working Paper, no. 13-027, August 31, 2012, Office for Scholarly Communication, https://dash.harvard.edu/bitstream/handle/1/9547823/13-027.pdf?sequence=1.

you can't be an expert at using your body language to influence your Outer Jury until you've mastered your Inner Jury. And just like with every other tool, once you've mastered your Inner Jury you can easily master the outer.

Presenting to Your Outer Jury

On to the fun stuff! So many people come to me for help on how to advocate on stage, on camera, or in conference rooms. They recognize that they aren't using their bodies, voices, and facial expressions to the best of their ability, and they want help. I help them—first by changing the way they present to their Inner Jury. Often that's enough. The change in the way they present themselves to themselves, and then receive, gives them more confidence. It gives them more joy. It makes their work so much more fun. When you're having fun your body and your tone change, so your audience knows it. When they know it, they start having fun, too, and they want more of what you're giving them. When it's time to present to your Outer Jury, you use the same tools.

Tone

Just as you can tell so much by receiving others' tones of voice, you're constantly giving to others with yours. I'll touch upon some of the recommendations I make to my coaching clients here. First, don't fool yourself into thinking you can't control your tone of voice. While it's true that an alto can't become a bass, there are ways to improve your tone and the way you speak.

1. *Stand up.*

   Posture impacts tone of voice. There's a reason you don't often see singers sitting. Standing opens up your posture and your lungs, allowing you to get your full breath and to use all that lung capacity. When you stand straight and tall, your voice will naturally improve.

2. *Slow down.*

   This is one I had to learn. The best listeners at trial are the court reporters. They're taking down every word every person in the courtroom says. Early in my career I had more than one court reporter ask me to slow down. I knew it was an issue, especially when I got excited or upset about what was going on in the case. My speed would increase with my enthusiasm. But one day a court reporter pulled me aside. Since the court reporter is responsible for taking down every word anyone says in court, I was making his job more difficult. I had to slow down and modulate my cadence. Once I started consciously considering the court reporter as I spoke, I naturally slowed down. I imagined that I was speaking directly to the court reporter, and that helped. You could try that, too. Imagine you're speaking to someone who has to type what you say, and it may help with your speed.

   Modulation is very important when it comes to tone. Very good advocates know when to speed up and slow down to ensure that their jury is not only listening to but also understanding what's most important. No matter what your tone of voice, you can use modulation to your benefit as well. When you slow down, you take more breaths. When you take more breaths, your voice naturally lowers and gets deeper. This will also help you to realize when you're getting carried away. I'll never forget the time early in my career that I won my first nonsuit. A nonsuit is granted by a judge when the plaintiff (in my trials that's the patient) has finished putting on her case but the defense (me and my doctor) has not yet begun with theirs. It's rare for a nonsuit to be granted in my cases, and I'd never seen it happen. But when the patient finished putting on her case, I felt like I had a strong argument for a nonsuit, so I prepared with laser focus. I'd definitely convinced myself, which got me a little excited and wound up to argue. I was arguing so vehemently that I wasn't noticing that I was winning. My client, the doctor, had to pull on my arm and whisper, "I think you've won," before I could slow down to hear the judge trying to interrupt me. If I'd been more modulated in my speech, I could have shut my mouth much sooner.

3. *Use your mind.*
   Some of my female clients have vocal habits they want to break. When those habits are really bad, I'll refer them to speech pathologists to help. But two of the most common bad habits can sometimes be broken with a little bit of consciousness. The first habit we often have to break is vocal fry. That's the habit of speaking from the back of the throat. The Kardashians have a reputation for doing this, especially Kim. And if you followed the story of Theranos and Elizabeth Holmes, you know she

also spoke with a vocal fry. Many believe women picked up this habit in an effort to sound more like men. But it is harmful to your throat and ineffective when you're advocating.

The other habit some of my coaching clients want to overcome is upspeak, which is the habit of ending declarative statements with a question mark at the end? Sort of like this? It sounds like a mix of Valley Girl and curious, but it makes the speaker sound unsure and not confident. Both of these habits have to go if you want to be a strong advocate for yourself and others.

Both of these habits can be addressed in the same way. Imagine that the words you're speaking are feathers. If you imagine sending those feathers out of your mouth and across the room, you will help to overcome vocal fry because you won't be holding the words back. Send your voice out with power and imagine the feathers shooting out of your mouth. And if you also imagine the feathers starting in the air and landing on the ground, your voice will often follow that trajectory. You'll break the habit of upspeak.

As an advocate you want to take advantage of everything you have available to you. Your tone is something you can optimize with just a little bit of consciousness.

Facial Expressions

Don't underestimate the impact a smile can have on your jury. There are a host of studies about the positive impact your smile has on others. One in particular showed that a person's physical attractiveness was directly and strongly influenced by the intensity of her smile.[23] Another researcher found that obituaries mentioned a loved one's smile more than any other attribute.[24] Your smile makes other people want to smile. And that, in turn, impacts their mood and their Inner Jury.

This was something I struggled with as a young attorney. I am naturally, and fortunately, a very happy person. I smile—a lot. In fact, I smile so much that it became a joke at depositions. I always brought water to depositions, and I found this brand of water (Fred Water) that was in a plastic bottle shaped like a flask. It fit perfectly in my bag and I didn't think anything of it until, more than once, the other attorneys at depositions would watch me pull it out to take a swig of water and say, "No wonder you're always so happy!"

But at trial I thought I had to hide my smile. My cases are usually sad. They often involve patients with catastrophic injuries, and I never wanted the jury to think I was taking that lightly. When you're talking about brain-damaged babies and paralyzed fathers, smiles are hard to come by. As such, I would never laugh or smile in the courtroom. Eventually I realized that was a mistake. As long as I was appropriately serious during the trial itself, it was okay to smile. In fact, the jurors and the parties

---

[23]   Jessika Golle, Fred W. Mast, and Janek S. Lobmaier, "Something to Smile About: The Interrelationship between Attractiveness and Emotional Expression," *Cognition and Emotion* 28, no. 2 (2014): 298–310, https://www.tandfonline.com/doi/abs/10.1080/02699931.2013.817383.

[24]   Marianne LaFrance, *Lip Service: Smiles in Life, Death, Trust, Lies, Work, Memory, Sex and Politics* (New York: W. W. Norton, 2011).

craved it after the seriousness of the case itself. The right smile at the right time can create a connection between me and a juror that I can't create any other way.

And the trials you might face don't usually involve such terrible stories. Most of the time when you're advocating to your Outer Jury, a smile is a wonderful tool. It makes you feel better. It makes them feel better. And it helps you win.

Body Language

When you're working to influence, persuade, or even convince your Outer Jury, body language helps. The more you can use it to your benefit, the better an advocate you'll be. I find that focusing on being open is key. Just like we talked about "owning it" in the Credibility chapter, you want to own your space. You want to have open shoulders, open heart, and open arms. I often find when I'm feeling stressed at trial, my shoulders start creeping up to my ears. When I feel that happen, it reminds me of a yoga teacher who said I often had "shoulders as earrings." I don't want that. It's not comfortable and it doesn't present a confident and sure picture to my jury. You don't want shoulders as earrings either. Do the work to put your Inner Jury at ease so that your Outer Jury can show it. Relax, open up, and present from that place.

In the Credibility chapter we also talked about the power of humility and how to embrace being grounded. You want your body to be grounded, too. The position of your feet, and what they're doing, can tell the jury a lot about you. Researchers believe that if your feet are pointed toward the door it's a signal that you want to leave. If your feet are bouncing and jiggling under the table, you're likely nervous. As I've mentioned, I think so much of it has to do with context and I have some friends whose feet are always jiggling and they're only nervous most of the time. But if you want to advocate with every advantage you can get, I'd recommend being aware of what you're doing with your feet. Ground them. Hold court. You've got this.

For me the most interesting part of body language when you're presenting to your jury is how you use your hands. In Joe Navarro's book *What Every Body Is Saying*, he talks about research showing that criminal defendants are found not guilty more often if they keep their hands on, and not under, the counsel table. When the jury could see their hands for most of the trial, they were more likely to win. Some lawyers believe this may be due to the lizard brain.

They say the lizard brain is the part of the brain that is focused on the four *F*s: flight, fight, food, and the other *F* word. Fornication. While recent neuroscience has disproven this lizard brain theory, there are some lessons that hold true. For example, some part of your Outer Jury wants to see other people's hands to make sure they aren't holding a weapon. It wants to know others aren't a threat, and when it sees their hands it feels just a little safer. That means that whether you're meeting with your Outer Jury face-to-face or on video, try to keep your hands visible. It's often a little harder on video. You have to arrange your camera so the picture includes your face and your hands when you move them. But it's especially worth it on camera. Your Outer Jury's brain is even more freaked out because it doesn't know how far away you are when you're on camera. That means it can't gauge the threat. Showing your hands will help put your Outer Jury at ease.

And using your hands makes you a more compelling advocate. You've already seen the story of the doctor who conducted an orchestra and won a case. I've seen similar situations time and time again. Juries liked witnesses who held themselves with the most confidence. They were open, grounded, and relaxed.

Your body often knows what to do even better than you do. Persuade your Inner Jury that you're credible, strong, and ready, and then trust your body to do its job. It will often gracefully lead you to your win.

Precedent

One of my clients sought me out after seeing me on television. I had been on the *Today Show*, and she was struck by the way I used my body language and tone of voice. Years later, the pandemic happened and suddenly she was presenting to her investors via Zoom rather than in person. Her ability to advocate on camera was of the utmost importance to her and her business. She wanted help.

We started by working on how her body language, facial expressions, and tone impacted her Inner Jury. She realized that her body followed her mind and her mind followed her body. The day that she recognized that she could control her mood with a shift in facial expression or posture, her face lit up. And then I watched her progress increase at warp speed.

She'd been comfortable presenting to her investors and potential investors across the boardroom table. But now she wanted to be just as comfortable on camera. We looked at her backdrop and her lighting. And we changed her camera placement to ensure that it maximized her ability to connect with her listeners. Then we got to practicing. She honed her body language, her ability to look straight into the camera as often as possible, and her tone of voice and modulation.

Since we've been working together, investments in her business have tripled. This is due in large part to her business model and her hard work. But she recognizes that good content is nothing without someone to advocate for it. She is that someone, and she's become one of the strongest advocates I know.

Summary of the Case: Presentation

1. *Your tone, body language, and facial expressions influence you as much as they influence others.* Your smile can make you happy, and your frown can bring you down. Be aware of the impact your body can have on your Inner Jury, and tap into that power as often as possible.
2. *Be aware of what your body, face, and voice are doing.* When you're excited, nervous, or aggravated you will likely lose that awareness and turn in to a squeaky talker with shoulders as earrings. But if you tap into

your presence and your breath before you advocate, you do have the power to control your presentation.

3. *Make people feel safe.* Your Outer Jury wants to feel safe. When you smile, speak slowly, and show them your hands, you're giving them what they want. And that's how you get what you want—and win.

Chapter 9
Negotiation

Know when you're negotiating.
And you're always negotiating.

From the minute your alarm goes off in the morning, you're negotiating.

Like everything you have just read, negotiating always starts with your Inner Jury. You always start negotiating with yourself first.

"I'll give you thirty more minutes of sleep for a workout this afternoon instead."

"If you take care of the kids this morning, you can get a sitter this afternoon."

"I'll focus on making money now, so that I can have kids later...or I'll have kids now and focus on my career later."

Your Inner Jury is always deciding, based on the better story and the better advocate. Facts tell, stories sell, and advocates win.

Then your negotiation moves on to your Outer Jury, the outer world. You negotiate with the other drivers to get ahead in traffic. I give, you give, I take, you take. When you start working, the negotiations continue.

"I can do the call at two o'clock."

"Three o'clock is better for me."

"How about two thirty?"

Then there are the larger-picture negotiations.

"I really want the opportunity to work with Sarah."

"I'd rather you work with me on this project."

"Well, if I agree to work with you on this one, can I work with Sarah on the Smith matter that's about to start?"

And if you have children, the negotiations never end.

"Brush your teeth and you can watch a show."

"Go to bed and I'll read you a story."

"Eat your peas and you'll get dessert."

Life is a constant negotiation because life is a give-and-take. And ultimately, that's all negotiation is. Advocates use words as tools, so we have to know where they come from and what they mean. The word *negotiate* comes from the Latin root "not leisure." Anytime you're not lying around doing nothing, you're negotiating.

Let's get good at it.

The Story of the Negotiation Gone Bad/Good/Bad

My cases often involve catastrophic injuries and extremely sympathetic patients. That is a deadly combination for a defense attorney. It gets even more difficult if you have a likable, sincere, young patient who lives and works in the community where the case is being tried. Every member of the jury can see life through the patient's eyes. They've all been patients, and many of them either look just like this patient or have brothers, uncles, sons, and partners who do. If, for example, this patient is paralyzed, disabled, or brain damaged, or he's had an amputation or a breathing tube inserted, then that means that he will never be the same. When the stories the patients' attorneys tell are this compelling, the defense attorney has to overcome the jury's natural ability to see things through the patient's perspective and the jury's natural inclination to feel sympathy for someone who is suffering. The defense attorney needs to ask the jury to instead focus on the dry medical experts and treatises that explain this type of horrific injury can happen even when everyone does everything right.

What patient wants to believe that?

These types of cases are almost impossible for the defense to win. As a result, we often try to settle cases where the damages are too horrible or the patient is too likable for the jury to see past it. That means I've been involved in a lot of negotiations.

One was very different.

Early in my career, the case involved a young woman who had pelvic surgery with my client and claimed that after the surgery she couldn't walk, have sex, or sit without pain. She'd had to get a stand-up desk for work because sitting for more than ten minutes caused excruciating nerve pain, and she'd had to stop her side hustle as a yoga teacher, which she loved. Her pain was so exquisite that she'd started taking strong pain medications and was concerned that she'd become addicted. Her anxiety had gone through the roof, so she had started taking antianxiety medications as well.

It was an interesting case because her damages were invisible. She was beautiful and young, but her eyes reflected her pain and the constant grimace on her face led to lines she never should have had at such a young age. When I took her deposition, I knew that she was telling the truth about her pain. I heard it in her voice and saw it in her eyes. But in my cases any settlement is paid by the insurance companies, and the woman from the insurance company thought she was lying. She wanted me to make the patient get additional nerve studies to prove that she actually had a problem. The patient's attorney had objected, arguing that the pain caused by these studies was unnecessary and inhumane. He noted that multiple doctors had documented that this pain was real. But the judge agreed with my half-hearted argument that we needed the studies. The patient complied, and the studies showed she had severe nerve injuries throughout her pelvis, which made pain shoot down both legs.

The doctor who had performed the surgery was confused and frustrated by the case. She'd performed thousands of similar surgeries and had never had a patient with this type of outcome. She believed she'd done nothing wrong. At the same time, she knew we'd have an uphill battle at trial. The jury would relate to the patient and not the doctor. They'd see the injury, the disability, and the tests we'd forced her to undergo through the perspective of the patient. We had no explanation to counter the patient's claim that the doctor had done something wrong. It was a case the doctor had been willing to settle from early on in discovery, and now that we had the nerve tests, the insurance company was willing to pay.

But it was difficult to get to mediation. The patient's attorney had been livid from the start. He'd been adamant that his client, the patient, should not have had to undergo that intrusive, painful study. He'd screamed at me about it and called me some choice names for filing the motion to compel it, despite knowing that I did so at the command of the insurance company that controlled the purse strings for the case. His ego was involved, and this made him not want to settle. He wanted to make the doctor pay for what she did to his client by getting a verdict against her, and he wanted to make the insurance company pay for the pain they'd put her through with a multimillion-dollar verdict. But verdicts take time. You have to go through the time and expense of trying the case, and he'd have to take the risk of losing and getting nothing for his client. Then, if he won, we'd likely find something to appeal, which would mean another year or so of no money for his client (or himself, as he got a third of his client's money).

Ultimately, he agreed to mediate the case.

Sometimes lawyers can negotiate a settlement on the phone or in person without any outside help. The patient's attorney will make a demand, and I'll bring it back to my insurance adjuster. She'll counter with a much lower offer, and back and forth we'll go until we reach an agreement and settle the case. But other times, we need help. Often help comes in the form of a mediator, someone who is trained in the art of negotiation. He brings the parties together in the same space and then practices shuttle diplomacy, going back and forth between the parties and attempting to find some common ground. The best mediators make it look easy and effortless, like a flowing dance, but having also been trained to be a mediator, I know it's hard and draining work. I knew we needed one of the best if we were going to get this case settled.

We hired him, and the day of the mediation I was praying he'd be able to make his magic work on this emotional group. The patient was there, despondent with pain and pacing the hallways to avoid sitting. Her attorney, on the other hand, sat in a chair and radiated anger and righteous indignation. My doctor—filled with confusion—was in the room with me. The insurance adjuster on the case was in our room as well, detached and clinical in her evaluation of the case.

All day long, we negotiated. At the start we were all in the same room, telling our stories to the mediator and for the benefit of the other side. Each attorney presented why they'd win the case in an attempt to make the mediator and the other side see things from our differing perspectives. The parties didn't speak. Then we went to different rooms, and the mediator traveled back and forth between us, bringing a demand to us and an offer back to the patient and her attorney. But at the end of the day we were still hundreds of thousands of dollars apart. My hopes that this case would settle were evaporating. Until the mediator proposed something unusual.

"I think we should let the patient and the doctor have a conversation, alone," he said.

This was an unusual request, though in my training I'd been told that it was an option if the mediation called for it. I wasn't sure that the risks would outweigh the benefits. We were still many zeros apart, and I wasn't sure that putting my client, the doctor, and the patient in the same room would help. What if the doctor said something that would hurt us? Conversations during mediations were meant to be protected, but there's never a guarantee. I was worried about my doctor. Over the course of the day she'd grown quieter and more withdrawn. She kept saying, "What will we do if it doesn't settle? I can't explain what happened here, Heather."

I trusted the mediator, so I was willing to agree to his request. The insurance carrier was hesitant but agreed, and the patient's attorney fought tooth and nail against it. But ultimately, we left the patient and her doctor alone in a room while the rest of us milled about by the coffee machine.

Less than an hour later, they came out. Their faces both seemed a little clearer and perhaps tear stained. Most surprising, though, was that they were both smiling.

"I'll take the offer," the patient said in a voice clear as a bell.

Her attorney sputtered and pulled her into a room. He came out later and said they weren't taking the offer that day, and he'd be in touch. After a lot more drama and a few days of additional negotiations, the case did settle for slightly more than our final offer that day.

Later, my doctor told me a little bit of what went on in that room after we left. She said she'd not opened her mouth except for twice. When the door closed, the doctor said, "I'm so sorry." The patient then poured out the details of her pain, and how the injury had impacted her life. She told the doctor about a boyfriend she'd lost because she could not make love, a yoga job she'd lost because she couldn't teach any longer, and all these dreams that she'd lost and couldn't recover. And my doctor listened, nodding, eyes filled with tears. Then the patient said, "I told my attorney that the money wasn't what mattered to me here. I wanted to get enough to make up for my side hustle, sure. But most of all I wanted to talk to you. I wanted to tell you why I had to sue you. I wanted you to hear it from me. That was my nonnegotiable."

When mediations work well, this is how they end. The patient felt that she'd spoken and been heard. The doctor felt the same. They both had the closure that a trial and a verdict usually can't give because of all the appeals. They had their questions answered, and they'd shared their evidence and their perspectives. Both the doctor and the patient had presented and received.

This negotiation can teach us a lot about how to negotiate for ourselves and with ourselves. And it reveals the two most important things to consider during negotiations—nonnegotiables and connections.

Negotiating with Yourself

You spend far more time negotiating with yourself and allowing your Inner Jury to decide than you'll ever spend negotiating with anyone else. What you gain from these negotiations is far more valuable than any raise, promotion, or better deal. Every time you negotiate with yourself and choose the option that's best for you, you're receiving more self-confidence, more self-awareness, and more understanding of where you can bend and where you will break. This knowledge is invaluable.

You are in a constant give-and-take with yourself. Make sure you know it. Because when you don't realize you're negotiating, you're likely to give up way too much.

When you're negotiating, know it. Make it a conscious decision. For example, every Monday I write down my calendar for the week, in hourly increments. That entire process is a negotiation. If I don't work out on Monday, I have to work out on Thursday. If I take that meeting on Tuesday morning at 10:00

a.m. that means my writing time has to switch to the afternoon. I'll get up at 5:00 a.m. every day so that I can feel and be my best. If I agree to that dinner date, I'm going to not want to work out the next morning. But since I'm already taking Monday off, I'm going to have to do it anyway. The entire process is one big, intentional negotiation.

But also set nonnegotiables for yourself. For example, my schedule is pretty nonnegotiable. Once I've committed to my week, that schedule becomes nonnegotiable. I do what I say I will do and don't have to take the time to wonder about it when the time comes. Nonnegotiables make mornings so much easier. My alarm goes off, and I don't negotiate with myself. I get up. My workout is scheduled, and I don't negotiate with myself. I work out. My nonnegotiables have led to many of my greatest accomplishments.

When I lost a lot of weight in college, I did it by taking away any possibility of negotiation. I gave up chocolate, potato chips, and cheese for years. It was easier for me to not have those foods than to negotiate with myself on amounts every time they were available. I made certain foods nonnegotiable. It made losing weight less of a struggle.

Nonnegotiables can save you. They save your time, your will-power, and your energy. When my alarm goes off in the morning, I don't even bother negotiating with myself about hitting snooze. Getting up at 5:00 a.m. is nonnegotiable. Working out on the days I've scheduled to work out is also nonnegotiable. I don't say, "Maybe tomorrow instead." I don't negotiate.

Until I do. There are times when I've had a rough night, fighting with insomnia, and when the alarm goes off, I'm a groggy mess. Then, rarely, I will say to myself out loud, "Let's renegotiate." This kind of self-talk, like the illeism/alter ego process in the Elegance chapter, is important. It makes me recognize that I am negotiating. It's intentional, thoughtful, and reasoned. And maybe in that moment I'll allow myself another hour to sleep in exchange for a midday walk. Or I might just say, "Let's negotiate. No workout today, and I'll double up on Sunday," and be done with it. The terms of the new negotiation aren't really what matters. What matters is that I know that I'm negotiating. It's thoughtful, not thoughtless. It's mindful, not mindless. It's a decision.

The same is true with decisions about work, opportunities, relationships, and food. If I've told myself I'll write from nine to eleven every morning this week, I do. And if a speaking or consulting opportunity comes up, I'll say, out loud, "Let's re-negotiate." Then I will. I make it intentional. Now I will write from one to three in the afternoon instead. Or I won't write that day, but I'll put in an hour on Saturday. It's an intentional negotiation, with new nonnegotiables. And that's the best way to have harmony between flexibility and rigidity. You have your nonnegotiables until you intentionally renegotiate. And only you can decide when that moment will be.

In that mediation, that patient had her nonnegotiable. She wanted to talk to the doctor. And her frustration with the mediation process, the pressure from her attorney, and the offer of tons more money didn't cause her to waver. She'd decided. It didn't mean she couldn't change her mind, but I got the feeling that it would have taken a lot to sway her. She was committed.

So intentionally set your nonnegotiables. Have them in your lifestyle, your relationships, your work, and your self-talk. Know what they are and set them with intention. And then know that it's okay to change them. Just do it with intention. Remember from the Credibility chapter. We make promises and we keep them. We set expectations and we meet them. And when we can't, we own it. Renegotiating your nonnegotiables is owning it.

Awareness and Connecting with Yourself

When you're negotiating with yourself, you have to know what you want. That means you have to know what you *really* want, and not what others have told you to want or what you think you should want. That requires self-awareness.

Self-awareness requires admitting some hard truths to yourself. Truths like you might want to have a child badly enough that you're willing to be with a partner you'd not otherwise have chosen. Or you might want to pursue your entrepreneurship dream badly enough that you're willing to give up a safe job and the security that comes with it. You've got to really know what's important to you, and why, in order to get it. And this takes time and a strong relationship with yourself. It starts with your elegance and ensuring that your Inner Jury is clear on what you really want. When that is clear, wanting more sleep, sugar, or sake will not take precedence.

Negotiating, even with oneself, means making connections, which takes the same effort that any relationship takes. You've got to spend time alone with yourself and your thoughts. You've got to listen to your intuition and your inner voice. If you never sit alone with yourself and your thoughts, you'll never know them. That's a problem, because then you'll never know what you really want. Other people's voices can easily drown out our own. Our inner voices that speak to our elegance tend to be the quietest. The only way you can be sure to hear them, especially in times of noise, distraction, and stress, is to be familiar with them. Know your inner voice and what it sounds like. Know what you want. Own your elegance. When you're deeply connected to yourself, the negotiation process becomes much easier. Those nonnegotiables are clear.

Negotiating with Others: Nonnegotiables

Mediators hate nonnegotiables. They get in the way of a settlement. If the patient's nonnegotiable is that the doctor must be fired from the hospital, that case is going to be tough to resolve. If the doctor's nonnegotiable is that the patient apologizes for suing him, we've got a problem. Nonnegotiables make a mediator's job difficult, and it makes it difficult for you when you're going to negotiate with someone else. When it comes to negotiating with others, I don't recommend that you have too many nonnegotiables. Instead, I recommend you identify your negotiables.

Let's imagine you're negotiating for a raise at work. You want $8,000 more a year, but your company is offering you $3,000. You're $5,000 apart, and no one is budging. What is another negotiable? If there are other things you want at work, you could focus on those things rather than money. For example, you might say, "I'll take the $3,000 if I can also work from home one day a week and get another week of vacation time." Or, "If I can leave at 3:00 p.m. on Monday, Wednesday, and Friday, we have a deal." Go past the dollar values and consider what else you're willing to negotiate. It might be time, title, or autonomy. You might want to negotiate for an opportunity you'd wanted, someone you want to work for, a title you'd like for your résumé, or a project you want to head. Be imaginative and come up with as many negotiables as you can before the negotiation.

In our mediation, the patient wanted to speak to the doctor as a nonnegotiable, but in some ways that nonnegotiable was also an additional negotiable. She wasn't only interested in money. She'd considered other things, and she wanted that meeting even more than she wanted additional money. It was a new negotiable the rest of us hadn't considered. But it worked for her. You need to know all the negotiables that work for you.

Once again, that means you have to be more self-aware. If you've already gone through a process of negotiating with yourself, you know yourself pretty well by now. You know what you're willing to accept and what you're not. Your boundaries are established, and you know which ones are written in chalk and which are written in stone. Allow your negotiables to grow out of that knowledge. You're much more likely to get what you want when you have a series of negotiables. It gives you room to move.

Negotiating with Others: Connection

My female clients often think they aren't good at negotiating. When they think of negotiation, they think of a used car salesman trying to get the best price for a car. And maybe you aren't good at that kind of negotiation. I know I wasn't. In fact, despite my training as a mediator and my twenty years of experience negotiating on behalf of my legal clients, I've always hated negotiating for myself. I'd avoid it at all costs, which meant that I often didn't get what I wanted because I didn't even try negotiating for it. I settled long before anyone even made an offer. And I've regretted it. Just like no one else can advocate for you as well as you can, no one else can negotiate for you either. You've got to do it for yourself.

Here are some tips on making the connections that will help.

1. *Ask for what you want.*

   For far too long, I assumed that people knew what I wanted. Part of this comes from too much empathy for others. I'm so tuned in to how others feel that I can't imagine that they aren't equally tuned in to how I feel. Most of the time I'm so aware of others that I know what they want from me before they ask. And I figure others feel the same. But they don't. When I was an associate attorney I spent many years not asking for the money I wanted. I thought that my partners should know all that I offered and should want to give me the money I thought I deserved. I went into my reviews waiting for them to bestow my raise on me like it was a blessing or a gift. As a result, I often left disappointed and feeling unappreciated. But I was wrong. It wasn't my bosses' job to figure out how much money I wanted and why. It was my job to tell them. And you have to do the same.

   Many of you are exquisitely tuned in to others' wants, needs, and feelings. That's a superpower. It makes you emotionally brilliant and very intuitive. But it can also make you a bad negotiator. You don't ask for what you want, because you think people either should know or do know what you want already. And you feel like if you ask, you're being pushy or greedy. It's almost like you think you're asking twice—once with your silent communication and once when you ask verbally. But just because you pick up on silent communications/intuition doesn't mean others do. They don't. If you don't ask, with your voice, loud and proud, they'll never know what you want, and then you'll never get it.

This can especially be a problem when it comes to romantic relationships. So many of us just assume our partner knows what we want. We don't want to appear to be needy or lacking in any way. We wait for our partner to offer us what we're silently negotiating for, and when they don't, we get angry. Save yourself and your partner. Ask for what you want. When you do, you'll have clarity and a connection. And that's the foundation for a win.

2. *Remember your alter ego.*
Negotiation is a form of advocacy. You've already hired yourself to be your best advocate. In the Introduction you created an alter ego whom you hired to ask for what you want and get it. You may have even decided on a transformation talisman to help. Put your alter ego to work now.

If you're about to negotiate for a raise, a car, or more respect from your partner, imagine the ideal negotiator. Would she be tough, strong, or even-handed? Would she be aggressive or calm? Imagine her in as many details as you can, and then hire her. Step into that persona. You can use a transformational talisman to help you make the transition, but then own that persona. If you do this every time you negotiate, you'll soon find that you no longer need an alter ego and that you've taken on all those attributes yourself.

3. *Patience is key.*

I struggle with patience. It's the main reason that even though I became certified to be a mediator I never pursued it as a career. I don't have the patience for it. A good mediator recognizes that an integral part of the process is the time it takes to change the parties' expectations. If you come into the negotiation expecting a million dollars, it will take time to get you comfortable with only getting $600,000. You can't rush that.

The other reason that patience is so important is that it allows for space between an action and a response. When your negotiation counterpart makes a lowball offer, you may be tempted to react. Your emotions may include anger, frustration, or fear. But if you allow for a little space to get past the reaction, you may find a response that includes calm, logic, or the ability to reach into your basket of negotiables. Emotions can be the death of a negotiation, and we let emotions get the best of us when we don't take the time to pause between a stimulus and a response.

I've had a handful of cases where we've had to have translators for the patients because they don't speak English. In those cases, the lawyer asks a question, then the translator translates it for the witness. The witness answers, in her native language, and then the translator translates. It is time consuming and boring. I've hated it at cross-examination, because there's so much time between my gotcha question and the answer that it loses its punch. But that pause is helpful in negotiations. You want any emotional issues to lose their punch. Great Japanese negotiators are rumored to bring a translator to a negotiation even if they speak perfect English. This allows them the time, while the translator is speaking, to craft a response rather than to react. That little bit of time can make the difference and allow for a more intentional response.

No matter whether you're negotiating with yourself or with someone else, you always want to be intentional. Know yourself first. Be aware of your trigger points, your wants, and your needs. But most of all, be aware of your negotiables and your nonnegotiables. You can't get what you want if you don't know what that is. And then you must be willing to ask for it.

Precedent

Marriage is one big negotiation, and, therefore, it's a great teacher. While I haven't been married, I've been in enough relationships to know that finding compromise in romantic relationships can be our greatest lessons and our greatest challenges. One of my clients used the end of his marriage to face both.

He was in a marriage that he called loveless and devoid of feeling. But he wasn't ready to leave. Staying made him miserable, but the thought of leaving made him stressed and scared of what his grown children would do. He stayed, and stayed angry, unhappy, and frustrated.

When he first hired me, it was to help him advocate at work. He had a new job with a new boss who was pushing back on many of his suggestions. He wanted to be a better advocate for his ideas. Over the course of our work together, though, he learned a lot about his negotiation style with himself, his wife and his boss. First, he learned that he didn't have many nonnegotiables for himself. He told himself his happiness was nonnegotiable, but he traded it for the comfort inherent in a lack of conflict. He told himself an honest relationship was a nonnegotiable for him, but he wasn't being honest about his feelings with himself, his boss, his wife, or his kids. I told him I didn't care what his nonnegotiables were. I did care whether he honored them. If he said something was nonnegotiable, then negotiating with himself every time it came up would hurt him. He'd lose his own credibility and then lose confidence in his ability to negotiate with others. He saw this happening in his life.

He began setting nonnegotiables and honoring them. He wanted happiness. But what would make him happy? He wanted honesty. He had to start being honest. And it all began at home. As he set nonnegotiables for his home life, his marriage actually started to improve. He realized that if he wanted happiness and honesty, he needed to do certain things to make that happen. And as he did, his relationship completely changed.

With every step forward in his relationship, his interactions with his boss improved. He and his wife went into counseling and started working on building a new marriage. His relationship with his children is better than it's ever been. And eventually, he left that job and started another at a higher salary with more freedom and more autonomy (all of which he negotiated for).

Summary of the Case: Negotiate

1. *You are always negotiating.* When you know you're doing it, you're bound to do it better.
2. *When you're negotiating with yourself, it's good to have nonnegotiables.* Otherwise you'll give in to yourself in moments of weakness. When negotiating with others, it's good to have a lot of negotiables. It gives you flexibility, and flexibility is key during negotiations.
3. *Be sure to pause.* Patience is a virtue in all aspects of advocating for yourself, but especially when you're negotiating.

Chapter 10
Argument

Misunderstanding is the enemy.

I've only been fired by a legal client once. Then he rehired me. And then I wanted to fire him. But the entire situation taught me more about advocating and argument than almost anything else I've ever experienced.

He was a fighter. This doctor was a surgeon who had achieved enormous success. He was also a boxer. He'd been practicing medicine for decades when he was sued for the first time. In our cases the insurance companies assign the attorneys to the doctors unless they have a specific preference. This doctor didn't have a preference, so he was assigned to me.

We got along fine at first. He was a lot like the other doctors I'd represented—confident in himself and his care, sure that he would win, and angry that he'd been sued. I met with him five times before his deposition. We met to initially review his care and the case process, and then four more times to dive deep into the records, the research about the surgery he'd performed, and his own research and writings on the topic. I knew no one could have prepared this doctor for his deposition as well as I had.

However, at the deposition things went south. The opposing attorney was a yeller and an instigator. His questions were meant to insult and to get the doctor riled up and emotional. The attorney had requested the deposition be videotaped so that when the doctor got riled up it would be there for the jury to see. The attorney would ask a question that any doctor would find extremely insulting, but he'd do it in a very placid voice and tone. Despite our preparation, the doctor would get somewhat defensive and angry, and it showed in his body language, his tone, and his energy. However, he was still answering the substance of the questions well due to our extensive preparation.

When the cameras weren't rolling, though, the opposing attorney was getting in my face. He was yelling about overdue discovery (that wasn't really overdue) and threatening to file motions (that I knew I would win). I smiled at him, poured more coffee, and asked him to get back to asking questions. I knew that despite the attorney's wrangling, my doctor was doing quite well.

My doctor didn't know that, though, and he wasn't happy.

"Why did you let him talk to you like that? Why did you put up with that?"

He wanted me to fight back. He was a fighter, and he was looking for a fighter.

"My goal isn't to fight. My goal is to win."

I knew that fighting with that attorney in that deposition wasn't going to get us any closer to a win. We weren't there to win the deposition. We were there to win the trial. And good answers would get us closer to a win. My doctor's feeding off my calm energy and not freaking out on camera got us closer to a win. We left that deposition that day closer to a win, and I knew it. That was all that mattered to me.

But it wasn't all that mattered to him.

He called my partner (an older male) the next day and said he wanted the partner to represent him. My partner got the insurance company involved, and it all culminated in a big meeting with my partner, me, the doctor, and a number of representatives from the insurance company. At that meeting I told the doctor no one knew the case as well as I did. I told him no one would be more prepared for trial, and no one would prepare him better. I assured him that I'd fight for him when and where it mattered, and I'd do everything I could to win. And if he'd rather go with my partner, I'd do everything I could to support them both.

He called me the next day and ordered me back on the case.

When we got to trial, I still didn't fight. When opposing counsel yelled and screamed at my witnesses, I quietly and calmly objected. When he got in my face in the hallway about refusing to settle, I smiled and moved past him. The doctor truly struggled with this. He still wanted me to fight. There were other doctors also being sued in this case, and my client would often tell their attorneys they were doing a great job (when they were yelling) but never commented on my work.

At the end of the case the jury found against the other doctors but not against my doctor. We won.

We'd won without yelling, without aggression, and without really fighting at all. We'd won with elegance, words, evidence, credibility, and questions. And we'd done it with reception and presentation and the occasional well-stated argument.

Argument is the last resort of an advocate. If you think you have to argue, I urge you to go back and reread all the other tools of an advocate. Try one of the others first. Because the times that you actually do have to argue are very rare. I believe the only time you want to argue is when there is one person or one body who decides who wins and who loses. If children are fighting over a TV show and the parents decide which show you'll watch, argument works. If your lawyers are fighting over a legal issue and the judge decides, argument works. And if you live in a condo and the condo board is going to decide where limited resources are going, argument might be the answer.

The only time to argue is when a third party decides. Otherwise, you're arguing with the person who will decide whether you win. And that's the key to a loss. That's the way to lose not only the argument but also the friendship, the client, the sale, or the opportunity.

Before you argue, start by asking yourself whether you need or want to be arguing at all.

Arguing When the Inner Jury Decides

As you know, your Inner Jury is the decider. It's the part of you that decides what to do, what to think, where to go, and what to believe. And sometimes you argue with yourself and the Inner Jury has to decide. It happened to me with that case with the doctor who wanted to fight. One part of me wanted to fight him. One set of voices in my head argued that I should tell him off and fire him as a client. They told me I didn't deserve this type of treatment and that I'd earned the right to be treated better. They argued loudly. Another chorus of voices said to go ahead and fight. If that's what he wanted, that's what he'd get. Even if it was bad for the case and bad for my client. But there was another voice that argued that the best thing to do was what had worked for me before. I had to stay calm. I had to stay focused. I had to recognize that the enemy wasn't my client or my opposing counsel. The enemy was actually misunderstanding.

The doctor's misunderstanding of the process and the jury led him to want me to fight and yell. My ego's misunderstanding of what was best for me and my ability to get more clients led me to want to fire him. But my Inner Jury had to decide which voices to follow. It had to be able to understand what it would take to win, what it looked like, and how to get there.

At the beginning of the book we defined *win* as "to receive something positive because you have earned it." The something positive I wanted in this case was a defense verdict for my client. I'd get it not by firing my client and not by fighting with the attorney. I'd get it by overcoming misunderstanding in the courtroom and helping the jury to understand. My Inner Jury understood all this and made the right choice.

When the voices inside your head, the different parts of you, start fighting, remember that you are not the enemy. Not one of those voices is the enemy. Misunderstanding is the enemy. Work to understand why those voices are fighting and what they need. Most of the time they can all get what they're looking for if your Inner Jury can stay calm and uninvolved in the drama. That makes you better at arguing to your Outer Jury as well.

Arguing to Your Outer Jury

The only time you should really be arguing with anyone is when a third party decides who receives limited resources. In the courtroom, the jury decides who will receive a verdict, and there's only one verdict to be had. In motion court, the judge decides who will win a ruling, and there's only one win to be had. In your life it may be that there's only one promotion to the role you seek, and you're arguing with the other candidates to receive that promotion. That is when you'll use the tool of argument to advocate.

The most critical part of arguing is *preparation*. You want to build your argument. There are two ways to have the tallest building in town. One is to knock down every other building. The other is to keep building your own. I think the best way to argue is not to focus on knocking down the other side or their argument. I think the best way is to build your own argument, brick by brick, from the ground up.

You start with *evidence*. You go through your body of evidence, the Win/Lose/Weird Process, and the 7X7W System just like we did in the Evidence chapter. Your evidence is the basis of your argument. You also prepare by seeing things from the Outer Jury's perspective. How does the decider (such as a manager, judge, or jury) see the argument, see you, and see your opponent? How do they see the world? You ask yourself these questions. And then you prepare with words and credibility.

Once you've prepared your argument, you have to be ready to make it. Here are three tips to help you make your argument.

1. *Be willing to be wrong.*

   If you start from a position where you're willing to be wrong, you're more likely to see the weaknesses in your own argument. That allows you to prepare for attacks. If you were an army general you'd want to see the holes in your defense so you can plug them. The same is true for your argument. Every argument has holes. Seeing them helps you fortify them.

   The willingness to be wrong also allows you to see where you might not need to argue. This happens often in our cases. By the time a case gets to trial, I've gone through all the processes you've gone through in this book until we arrive at the stage where argument/trial is our last resort. But it still isn't the only resort. Settlement is still an option.

   Just because my doctor/clients want to settle their case doesn't mean the case will settle. Often, the patient's attorney wants more money than the insurance company is willing to pay, so we have to go to trial. But even once trial starts, negotiations continue. I have to explain to my clients that just because we've chosen a jury doesn't mean the case won't settle. In fact, once the jury is chosen, one side often recognizes that a particular jury is going to have a much easier time seeing things through the doctor's perspective or the patient's perspective. Cases often settle right after jury selection. Or during openings there may have been three jurors crying at the story of the patient's damages. This, too, may make the case easier to settle. Trials go on like this. Open, negotiate, and maybe settle. Cross-examine a witness, negotiate, and maybe settle. Lose a motion, talk settlement.

This was one of the hardest things for me as a young trial attorney to understand. When you're negotiating, you're looking at compromise and all the weaknesses in your case. When you're in trial, your goal is to win, so you don't want to focus on where you could lose. But you must. Wearing the hats of a negotiator and an arguer is challenging. But it's only when you're willing to be wrong that you can be sure to do what's right for your client, your case, and your win.

I've tried a number of cases against a trial attorney who never seemed to see the weaknesses in his own case, and I've beat him every time. Eventually, we became friends, so I asked him whether he sees the weaknesses in his cases when he goes to trial. He said he was "often wrong, never in doubt." He felt that he had to blindly believe in everything that he was saying to win. That didn't work for him, and it won't work for you. I think a better mantra is "often right, always curious." That's how I win.

2. *Let the Outer Jury create the win.*
   Remember the origami study? That research showed that the participants put a higher value on origami that they created. People like their own creations and ideas. People want to feel good about giving out wins. This is especially true in those situations where there truly is an argument. Unless the jury/judge/manager/decider really dislikes one side or one argument, they usually have a

hard time letting the other side down. When you tell them they have to do it and how, you run the risk of getting less than you otherwise would.

For example, in my cases the patient's attorneys are asking for money. That's the only recourse available to injured patients. Some attorneys will take time during their case to add up all the losses to the patient. They'll have economists come in and testify about past lost wages, future lost wages, past medical bills, future medical bills, and what the monetary value is of work that the injured patient did around the house or for the family. Then we defense attorneys have to cross-examine those witnesses to try to reduce those numbers.

I hate it. I hate even talking about damages and money. The jury only gets to money discussions if they've decided my client was negligent. It's only after they've determined that my client is to blame for the injuries that they start to consider how much the patient should get to be compensated for the injuries. I never want them to get there. But if they do, I certainly don't want to tell them how much to award. The jury doesn't want me to either.

In my experience, it's the patient's attorneys who let the jury decide who get the highest verdicts. If the patient wins a case under the law she is to be compensated for her lost earnings, medical bills, and loss of services but also to be compensated for her pain, her suffering, her "embarrassment and humiliation." How do you put a price on such things? And how do you tell other people how to do that? You can't. You have to let them decide. Those attorneys who recognize that always get more money—the jury wants to create its own verdict. They want to create the win.

Let your Outer Jury create your win. Tell them what you want, of course! But leave room for their imagination. Leave room for them to add their life experience, their perspective, and their evidence to your win. Sometimes your manager, your investor, your client, or your customer can come up with a better win than you ever could have imagined. You'll find that when your Outer Jury contributes to your win they'll also help you keep it. They'll help you grow it. They now have a piece of the ownership of that win, and that makes it their win as well. That's when they become your best advocates.

3. *Misunderstanding is the enemy.*
Your opponent isn't your enemy. This is one of the hardest lessons for my legal clients to understand. I find in times of conflict people look for enemies. It's a lot easier to shoot down a bad guy than to overcome an *-ism*, or an idea. But if you're looking for the real wins and the true change, the enemy usually isn't just one or two people. The enemy is misunderstanding. And when you vanquish that enemy, you win forever.

That is why I never attack the other side. I most definitely never attack the patient. There are times when opposing counsel is so treacherous and so conniving that I'll point it out to the jury for them to come to their own conclusions (and create their own origami). But I'll never attack the patient. I will take their story, but I'll never take their dignity. I encourage my legal clients to approach the trial the same way.

The jury doesn't want to hate. They want to understand. If we truly believe we're right, then our job isn't to make the other side wrong. Our job is to help the jury understand why we're right. That takes more patience. It often takes more creativity. I like to picture misunderstanding as an actual thing. It's dark and mean and brooding. For me it looks a little like Jabba the Hutt. Our job at the trial is to kill misunderstanding. We do it with the ten tools of an advocate.

If your client is leaning toward choosing your competitor, it means they misunderstand why your offering is so much more fitting for them. An investor who might give their money to another start-up doesn't understand why yours will yield a greater return. A boss who could give someone else the promotion you want needs to understand how you will serve her and the business better than anyone else. Your job is not to beat the competitor. Your job is to make her understand—to fix the misunderstanding.

One of my favorite moments in all my trials was when I felt the jury's understanding. It was a complicated medical case, and I was cross-examining the patient's expert. That expert was relying upon misunderstanding to help his side win, making everything very confusing and convoluted, and then inserting a simple statement like, "If the doctor had done X, the patient would have lived." More confusion, more chaos, more curse of knowledge, and then, "If the doctor had done *X*, the patient would have lived." And it was working.

The patient's attorney finished his examination of his expert late in the afternoon on a Wednesday, and I had to begin my examination the next morning. The last thing their expert said that Wednesday afternoon was, "If the doctor had just done the right thing, Mr. Smith would have lived." Super. I had my work to do. I had to beat misunderstanding.

That night I laid out all the hundreds of medical articles I'd read on the topic in the case on my floor. Each one of these articles made it clear to me that the patient's underlying and unknown condition had killed him. But I had to make that clear to the jury. I took the main point from each one and broke the curse of knowledge. I made sure every word that I used was a word this jury, with their education and their life experience, would understand. I then turned the point into a yes-or-no question. I would read the statement and ask the expert if he agreed. If he said yes, great and on to the next question. If he said no, I'd show him the line from the article that said the same thing (in more complicated language). He'd have to disagree with the article and not with me. I knew I'd have to do this slowly, because confusion and misunderstanding move much more quickly than clarity.

The next day, that's what I did. Statement by statement, I asked the expert to agree or disagree. When he went off-track, I imagined misunderstanding dragging him away and I dragged him back. I slowed down, not just with my modulation but with my body language. I walked more slowly to my lectern. I took a pause after his chaotic answers. And then I'd follow up.

Slowly, I watched the jury understand. Their body language changed, their facial expressions changed, and their energy changed. They were leaning forward, nodding their heads, taking more notes, and looking at me more closely. I was about three-quarters of the way through my examination when the judge interrupted my flow.

"Ms. Hansen, is this a good time to break for lunch?"

Ugh. This moment is the worst. You don't want to break for lunch, because you're in a flow and it will give the witness time to gather himself and rearm for battle. But you don't want to make the judge angry either by telling her no. Even more importantly, you don't want to make the jury angry if they are dying to eat/take a break/go to the bathroom. Different lawyers handle this differently. Some say, "I only have ten minutes," (when they really have forty) and just keep going. I tend to err toward, "The jury wants lunch."

I was about to acquiesce when one of the jurors spoke.

"Let her finish."

That rarely happens. Jurors aren't supposed to speak up like that in court. They're only supposed to communicate with us after the evidence has all been presented, and then through the foreman. But this juror was clearly into it. She was starting to understand, and she wanted that to continue. Other jurors then whispered, "Yeah," and "Let her finish."

A friend of mine was in the courtroom that day, and once we did break for lunch, he told me the minute the juror said, "Let her finish," he knew I'd won the case. I never jinx myself by thinking that way, but I did know one thing for sure. Together, the jury and I had beaten misunderstanding that morning. They did it with their attention, and I did it with my research, my preparation, my presentation, and my reception. I did it with the tools of an advocate.

Your enemy is always misunderstanding as well. When you're in conflict with your team member, your client, your boss, or your family member, it serves you to remember that that person isn't your enemy. Chances are you'll have to work with that person again. Ideally, you want to turn that person into an advocate. The way we turn adversaries into advocates is by never looking at them as adversaries. Look at your adversaries as potential allies in the fight against misunderstanding, and you're closer to a win.

This is hard. Humans like to find enemies, and we prefer enemies we can see. That's why fighting racism, sexism, and poverty isn't as satisfying as fighting bad cops, Harvey Weinstein, and specific capitalists. It's easier to fight when you have a target you recognize. But that fight will have to be repeated, again and again. If you're in a fight with your team member, you might win that fight. But if you haven't overcome the misunderstanding that led to the fight, it's just going to repeat itself. The same is true with your arguments with managers, investors, family, students, and patients. Remember that misunderstanding is the enemy and you might beat it as allies.

Rejection

When your jury rejects your argument, they're not rejecting you.

This lesson took me a very long time to accept. Losing is exquisitely hard for me, as it is for most of us.

The first time I lost a trial, I didn't see it coming. I should have. It was type of case we tried to settle ahead because the patient was so sympathetic and the medicine was so hard to explain. But sometimes you know your argument so well and live it for so long that it's hard to see the weaknesses. I'd started the preparation for this trial knowing it was a case we were likely to lose. But the doctor didn't want to settle, so we were trying the case to verdict. There'd be no mid-trial settlement discussions in this trial, so I went all in. I believed, my client believed, and we believed so strongly that we were both gobsmacked when the jury came back with a verdict for the patient. We'd lost. Our story, and our advocacy, had been rejected. And by that I mean I'd lost. My story, and my advocacy, had been rejected.

Prior to that day I'd seen all my many wins as my clients' wins. (They were such good witnesses! They really connected with the jury!) But this time, I saw this loss as mine. (My opening stunk. My cross-exams were weak.) I felt personally rejected. As I stood outside City Hall, fighting tears, one of the jurors approached me.

"We just really wanted her to have some money and start out fresh." Then he walked away.

At the time I was grateful for the reassurance, but I still didn't believe him. It had to be something I'd done or not done, said or not said. It was my job to control the outcome. I continued to feel that way for another fifteen years. Every trial was a measure of my abilities as an advocate. Most of the time I won, and I attributed that to strong clients and charismatic witnesses. But when I lost, the jury had rejected me.

That attitude is part of what led me to my mini breakdown in the car that day. But it is also what led me here—to this fabulous second career sharing the tools to help people like you advocate for themselves. Because when losing an argument is losing yourself, there's just far too much on the line.

Finally, I was able to recognize that no one can reject me but me. My Inner Jury is responsible for deciding whether to believe in me, in the work I've done, and whether I've given my all. Any outside rejection is about a host of things—that jury, that client, that set of facts, that argument. Of course, I have a piece to play. But I'm not the only piece.

If you can remember that a rejection of your argument isn't a rejection of you, it will make you a better advocate. You'll have more confidence, more playfulness, and less attachment to outcome. You'll recognize that argument is the last tool of an advocate, and since you're not defending your very existence, you can use the other tools first. You'll see argument as the last resort, meant only to vanquish misunderstanding.

Precedent

A client I was coaching was dealing with a lot. She started a business that became very successful, but then she had a falling-out with her business partner. She wanted to divest from the partnership, so she hired me to help her advocate throughout the process.

She was an ideal client. She studied all the tools I offered her and did the work. She was religious about it. First, she worked on her Inner Jury, and then she moved on to the Outer Jury—her partner. Still, her partner wouldn't budge on anything. Every time my client saw things through her partner's perspective, her partner didn't return the favor. Every time my client asked questions, her partner stonewalled her. Eventually, after months of trying, they had to take their argument to court. And when the judge ordered them to mediate, my client was ready to negotiate. But her partner was not. The partner didn't want to mediate. The partner wanted to go to trial—an argument was going to be the only way to resolve this disagreement.

My client was frustrated. She felt as though she'd
done all the work with me for nothing. Until the trial
began. It was during trial that she recognized that all the
work she'd done with her Inner Jury had given her credibility, perspective, and the words that helped her cause.
She had presentation and reception skills that served her
throughout the two-week trial. When the trial was over
and the argument was decided, my client got every single
thing she'd asked for. She'd advocated her way to a win.

Summary of the Case: Argument

1. *Argument is the last resort.* You want to try all the
   other tools of an advocate before you reach for argument. Because the danger of argument is that
   you risk winning the argument and losing the sale,
   client, or relationship.
2. *Misunderstanding is the enemy.* People will often want
   to find a human to blame. It makes it much easier to
   hate and attack. But your goal is to help your Inner
   Jury and your Outer Jury understand.
3. *Let rejection be.* Let it be about something other than
   you. Let it be there, without making you crazy, anxious, or stressed. Let it be part of life, and let it be
   about too many things to count. It's not about you.
   You just don't have that kind of control.

190

Conclusion: Ending with Elegance

It's all a choice.

You are the advocate you've been waiting for. You advocate every time you ask for support, money, or time. You advocate when you sell, when you intervene, and when you make a request. Now you have the tools to do it well.

I work with individuals like you to help you become your own best advocates. But I also work with corporations, health systems, and other businesses to create entire advocacy curriculums for their teams. They learn the tools to advocate for themselves, their products, their plans, and their ideas. And that work is based on the foundation of the 5 Cs of an Advocate. I want to leave you with those 5 Cs as your foundation as you put the tools you've learned into practice.

The 5 Cs of an Advocate

1—Connection

In order to advocate well, you want to connect with your jury. You can do this with Words—by overcoming the curse of knowledge and using words that speak to your jury. And you do it with Questions, by finding out what your jury wants and needs to hear. Reception and Presentation are also great ways to connect. Once your jury starts mirroring you, you know you've made connections.

Connections are key for an advocate, because once you've connected you're on your way to a win.

2—Compassion

The definition of compassion is "a strong feeling of sympathy and sadness for other people's suffering or bad luck and a desire to help." It's the desire to help, and actually putting that desire into action, that defines compassion for an advocate.

It's not enough to see things from your jury's perspective. You have to put what you see, that new perspective, into action. It's not enough to collect Evidence or ask Questions, you've got to put what you get into action. Compassion is combining the heart and the mind of an advocate and using them to start advocating. And you can't advocate well without it.

3—Creativity

An advocate can use her creativity with every one of the tools. Every choice of word can be creative. Every Question, every way that you use Evidence, your Negotiables (and nonnegotiables) and your choice of

Argument all reflect your creativity. Being an advocate is meant to be fun. Use your creativity and make it so.

4—Curiosity

As you know, I love Questions. I think they're magic, and that means curiosity is magic. As an advocate, you want to be curious about your jury's perspective (and how you can change it). You want to illustrate that curiosity through your Questions and how you examine your Evidence. You want to be curious about the other side's Argument (if you reach that stage). Curiosity may have killed the cat, but it crowns the advocate.

5—Credibility

Whenever I share the 5 Cs with my corporate clients, inevitably someone asks, "Which C is most important?" I tell them, without hesitation, "Credibility."

You can't win unless they believe you. And you can't make them believe unless you do. You use every one of the ten tools when you are building Credibility, and the misuse of any one of those tools can lead to a loss of Credibility. If you only focus on one C, and you only focus on one tool, focus on Credibility. Believe. Then bring your jury along for the ride.

Now you have all of the ten tools you need to Advocate to Win. You have the 5 Cs of an advocate. But I'd like to end with one more C. Choice.

Because you are the angel you've been waiting for. You're your own best advocate, and you are the key to all your wins. It all rests on your choices. As such, we end where we began—with elegance.

Your elegance is your choice. You make your choices, and your choices make your life. Different choices, different life. If you look back at every one of the tools I've shared in this book, they're each a choice. You choose your Words—whether you're speaking them to your Inner Jury or your Outer Jury. You choose your Perspective. You choose your Questions, and whether to answer them. Your Evidence, how you Receive, your Presentation, and how you Negotiate or Argue—each a choice. I want to impart to you the three-step technique I share with my clients to help them make their best choices.

Three Steps to the Elegance Technique

Step One: Know that you're choosing.

Every moment of every day, you make choices. You choose whether to snooze or to get up with the alarm (which you chose to set the night before). You choose which side of the bed to get up on (literally and figuratively). You choose whether to brush your teeth, and how you'll greet the first person you see. Then you choose what you eat, whether to work out, and what you will do with your day.

You also choose your thoughts. This notion is a little harder for my clients to accept. If you think back to the STEER process that I shared in the Perspective chapter, you remember that it is made up of Sight, Thought, Emotion, Enaction, Result. First you choose what you See. There are always a number of ways of looking at a situation, and how you see something impacts your Thought. And you do choose what you think. This is the greatest gift we have as human beings—we choose. But for many of my clients it's also the greatest burden. If they choose what they think, and that impacts how they feel, then they're responsible for how they feel. And if they're not feeling great, that is a tough pill to swallow.

But it shouldn't be. Because it means that you always have the power to choose differently. And the best choices are made when we know that we're choosing. Some choices are better made unintentionally. Whether to snooze or rise and whether to brush your teeth are good examples of choices that you no longer have to know that you're making. When you make those things into habits, it frees up your human brain to make the choices that matter. So now you can choose whether to greet your partner with a kiss or a complaint. You can choose whether to do yoga or watch the news. And you can choose whether to see the day as an opportunity or a problem.

Self-awareness is one of the most important attributes you can cultivate. Studies show that when we see ourselves clearly, we are more confident and more creative. We make sounder decisions, build stronger relationships, and communicate more effectively. We're less likely to lie, cheat, and steal. We are better workers who get more promotions. And we're more effective leaders with more satisfied employees and more profitable companies.

I believe that self-awareness begins when we see that we're choosing. That kind of awareness can come from meditation. It can come from journaling or yoga. It definitely comes when you get a good coach. But it also comes from practice. Every time you make a choice, note that you're making it. Write it down, put it in your phone, or tell it to your partner.

"I'm choosing to stop working at five o'clock tonight."

"I'm choosing to see this as a crisis," or "I'm choosing to see this as an opportunity."

"I'm choosing to leave," or, sometimes harder to accept, "I'm choosing to stay."

When you know that you're choosing, you take your power back. You carve away some of the marble.

One of my clients struggled with this. She'd just started a new job and felt the stress of wanting to impress her team. But she also wanted to meet a partner and was actively dating. She'd met someone she really liked, and they had plans to go to dinner for the first time after weeks of phone calls and texting. They went on the date, and she was having a phenomenal time. Until her phone rang, and it was work. She answered. From there, the date went downhill, and she hadn't heard from him since.

When she told me the story, I stopped her there. "Do you see that you chose to answer?"

"No. I had to answer. It was someone working with me on a big project, and I had to make sure everything was okay."

She said it as though she was telling me the Earth is round. But answering wasn't a given—her thought and her action were a choice. And until she saw that she was choosing, she'd continue to give up her power. We worked on it. Over time she started to see when she was choosing (and that she was always choosing). Most importantly, she started to see there were situations in which she wanted to make choices, intentionally and with awareness that she was choosing.

In time, she met someone new whom she really liked. And when the time came for her first date, she told me she'd made some choices about the date. She chose what she was going to wear and which perfume she'd dab on her neck on her way out the door. And she chose that she wasn't going to check her work emails or take work calls during the date. To me, that was the most important choice. She was choosing herself, her needs, and this potential relationship over a work issue that likely could be handled later. And that choice would matter far more to her date than her outfit or her perfume. And it has. They're now married. My client continues to choose one night a week when she turns off her phone and turns on the romance.

Know you're choosing and your choices might change.

Step Two: Know who is choosing.

This is where your Inner Jury comes in to play. She is the one that chooses. For many of my clients, their greatest a-ha moments come when they realize that their Inner Jury isn't there to judge them. She's there to choose. The judgmental thoughts are coming from one set of voices in the brain. But there's another set of voices, even if they're faint, that are encouraging and loving. (And if they aren't loud enough, we work on that, too. Soon, they speak up.) Their Inner Jury isn't the judgmental voices. She's the one who chooses whether or not to listen to those voices.

Your Inner Jury is the one making your choices. And I've found it helps to picture her. For me, my Inner Jury is me forty years in the future. I picture her—gray hair in a low pony, starched white shirt with a little pop in the collar, black leggings, and the coolest sneakers ever. She's often watering plants on a terrace overlooking a city (which is a little weird since I do *not* have a green thumb, but maybe she does). When my Inner Jury makes choices, they're to serve her. Will this work make her happier, richer, smarter, or more fulfilled? Will this food make her healthier, leaner, more agile, and pain free? Will this relationship bring a sparkle to her eye, even if it's because of a memory? My Inner Jury knows things I don't. I listen to her when I choose.

I encourage my clients to create a visual of their Inner Jury as well. Most of them choose what I've chosen—themselves in the future. They dress her, give her a setting, and check in with her when they're choosing. This helps them be aware that they're choosing (Step One). And it helps them be aware of who is choosing.

Because other parts of you can choose. Habit sometimes chooses. For example, the time you get up, the side of the bed you get up from, and brushing your teeth are all habits you may have in the morning. And whether you kiss your partner or complain about the day—habit may be choosing that one, too. But if your Inner Jury were choosing—would she choose differently? It makes sense to have habit choose the basics. In fact, in an interview by Michael Lewis for *Vanity Fair*, President Obama said that he had the same thing for breakfast every day and always wore blue or gray suits because he "had too many other decisions to make."[25] He let habit choose those things, so he could choose others. Steve Jobs famously always wore turtlenecks, perhaps in part for the same reason. When habit is choosing the easy stuff, your Inner Jury has more capacity for the rest.

---

[25]   Michael Lewis, "Obama's Way," *Vanity Fair*, October 2012, https://www.vanityfair.com/news/2012/10/michael-lewis-profile-barack-obama.

Sometimes ego chooses. Sometimes it's fear. For my client who answered the phone on her date, it was a little of both. She wanted to be seen by her colleagues as capable and available, and she was afraid of losing her job. In my experience with hundreds of clients, fear and ego don't choose well. And they often choose most frequently. But when you can become aware of who is choosing, you can start giving the job to your Inner Jury. That's where it belongs.

Step Three: Know, and like, your reasons.

This is my favorite part of the Elegance Technique. It helps my clients to prevent all the second-guessing and stress they often engage in over their choices. And if you can start to know and like your reasons, you will find it will do the same for you.

So often, the reason you struggle with choosing is because you are afraid of making the wrong choice. Instead, you don't choose at all. You talk about it, cry about it, and suffer over it. And nothing gets done. But the truth is this: *there is no such thing as a bad choice.* I said it. There's no such thing as a bad choice. All there is are bad reasons.

You'll never know whether a choice was good or bad. You don't know what will happen one year, five years, or five hundred years from now. The choice you just made may impact future generations in ways you'll never realize. So perseverating and ruminating on whether a choice is good or bad is not helpful. It wastes time, resources, and energy.

Instead, there is a better way.

Rather than going round and round about your choice, try listing your reasons for your choice. List all the reasons you'd make for one choice. Then list all the reasons you'd make for another. Look at your lists and choose the reasons you like best. That's your choice. And then—don't look back. Make your choice, like your reasons, and let that be enough.

We did this for my client who chose to turn off her phone for her date. Her list of reasons for keeping her phone on looked like this:

> To feel less stressed about work (fear).
> To be sure I don't miss anything (fear).
> To be available to my boss if she needs me (fear).
> To impress my boss (ego).

Her reasons for turning the phone off at 6:30 p.m. when the date began:

> To be present on my date.
> To get to know him, without distraction.
> To ensure he knows that this date is important
> to me.

She liked her reasons for turning the phone off. And no matter what happened—even if there was a big catastrophe at work—she knows that she'd liked her reasons and that was enough.

I learned the importance of liking my reasons in the courtroom. I didn't lose often, but when I did, I could second-guess every choice. *I shouldn't have used that witness, that exhibit, that analogy.* I'd torture myself for days with the choices I could have made. But once I developed my Elegance Technique, that changed. And when I liked my reasons for a choice I made at trial, I stopped second-guessing myself. I reminded myself that I liked my reasons and why. And it was easier to move on.

Winning

To win is to receive something positive because you've earned it. This is good news because it means you choose your wins. I learned that from one of my courtroom losses. The case involved a delivery of an infant, though the baby was fine. The mother was fine, too, but years later she developed complications and alleged it was due to something that happened during the delivery. When I took the young mother's deposition, I asked about her life, her hopes, and her dreams. Her child was now four years old, smart, and precocious. I remember the smile in her eyes as she spoke of him.

When we got to trial, I put on my warrior armor and got to work. I represented two doctors who had done the exact same thing in the case. However, I could tell that the jury found one of the doctors credible and the other not so much. His body language was more nervous, his tone more arrogant. He chose words that didn't resonate as well and argued a little too much with opposing counsel. I was getting concerned.

Then the jury went to deliberate. And they were taking too long. In general, the quicker the jury comes back with a verdict, the better for the defense. It means they aren't taking time to add up numbers and look at damages. And this was starting to look like maybe they were. I went to work negotiating. I spoke to the doctors, the insurance company, and opposing counsel about agreeing to a high/low in the case. That meant that no matter how high the verdict, the patient wouldn't get more than the agreed-upon high. But it also meant that even if she lost, the young mother would get something: the low. We negotiated the numbers, and I included a provision that if the doctors lost, we'd keep the loss confidential, meaning no press. We reached an agreement.

Within an hour of our shaking hands, the jury came back. They'd found against one of my doctors and for the other. That verdict made no sense factually but showed the power of a strong advocate. The number the jury awarded was right in the middle of our high/low. And the case was over.

At first, I still considered it a loss. It was a loss for that doctor, and he felt it. I was morose, in tears, and angry with myself. Then I used the Elegance Technique. One: know you're choosing. I was choosing to see this as a loss. I was choosing to mope and berate myself. And that meant I could make another choice. Two: know who is choosing. Here it was my ego, for sure. Also, my fear that the doctor would tell other doctors I was a bad attorney. But if my Inner Jury chose, what would she choose? She'd choose to find the lesson here. And so I did. I looked at ways this case could have gone differently. But I also chose to see this loss as a win. First of all, I'd sensed that the jury was going to find against us. And I used that intuition to negotiate a fabulous resolution that protected my clients. I'd actually done well. And as for the mother, maybe she'd use the money she received to educate her young son. Maybe he would have a completely different life as a result. And maybe he'd go on to find the cure for cancer. That new perspective gave me peace. Three: know your reasons. I was choosing that story, that perspective, because it helped me let go of beating myself up. It allowed me to move on and to serve the next client. I liked my reasons.

When that case was over, I received something positive. I received a new perspective. I received peace and a sense of pride. I received more faith in my intuition. And I earned it by choosing.

Your Turn

You earn your wins, too. You make your choices, and your choices make your life. Then you advocate for those choices.

It's time for you. Start by helping your Inner Jury make the choices that will best serve your life. Choose better relationships. Choose better health. Choose more money. Choose a new career. Choose to be the angel in the marble. Choose your highest potential. And then—advocate. Advocate to your partner for more communication and better understanding. Advocate for more time to work out and prepare (or in my case buy) healthy meals. Advocate for that raise. Advocate for that opportunity.

Choose yourself, and then advocate for yourself. When the Inner Jury believes, the Outer Jury will follow.

It's your turn.

Go out and win.

Be an advocate.
Don't be better
Be better